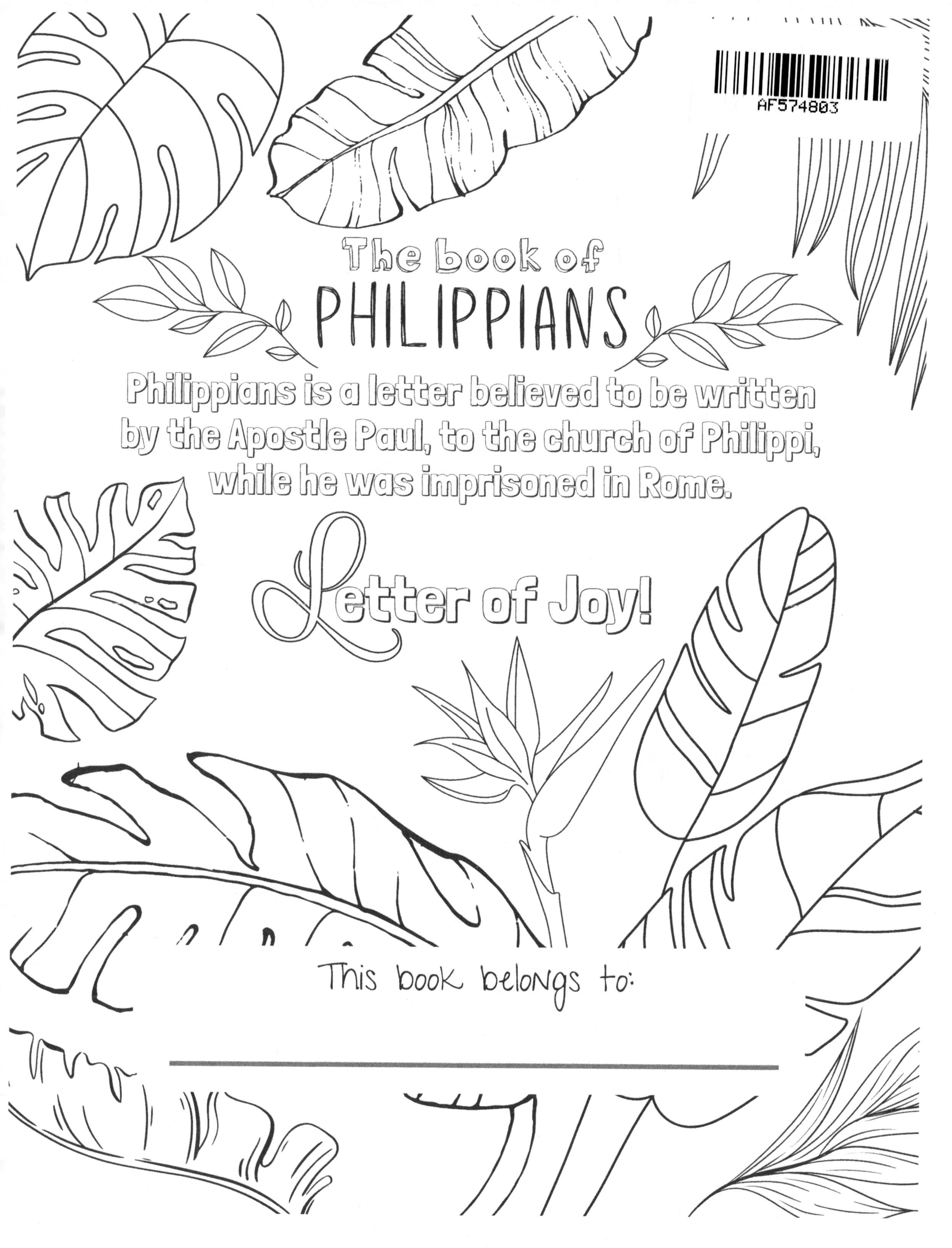
AF574803
The book of
PHILIPPIANS
Philippians is a letter believed to be written
by the Apostle Paul, to the church of Philippi,
while he was imprisoned in Rome.
Letter of Joy!
This book belongs to:

Bible Color Therapy - Philippians: Plants
Copyright © 2025 Amanda Kiser

All rights reserved. No part of this publication may be reproduced, distributed, or transmitted in any form

or by any means, including photocopying, recording, or other electronic or mechanical methods, without

the prior written permission of the publisher, except in the case of brief quotations embodied in critical

reviews and certain other noncommercial uses permitted by copyright law. For permission requests, email

Bloom Publishing, addressed "Attention: Permissions Coordinator," at paula@bloominthedark.com.

Published by Bloom Publishing, an imprint of Bloom In The Dark, Inc.

Title: Bible Color Therapy - Philippians: Plants

Paperback edition, Published March 21, 2025

ISBN-13: 978-1-951558-02-4

www.bloominthedark.org

Scripture references are limited quotes from the online versions of these Bibles:

Scripture quotations marked "ASV" are taken from the American Standard Version Bible (Public Domain).

Scripture quotations marked (WEB) are taken from the WORLD ENGLISH BIBLE, public domain.

Scripture quotations taken from the Amplified® Bible (AMPC), Copyright © 1954, 1958, 1962, 1964, 1965, 1987 by The Lockman Foundation.

Scripture taken from the New King James Version®. Copyright © 1982 by Thomas Nelson. All rights reserved.

Credits

Some elements sourced from Canva.

FOR MORE CREATIVITY:
WWW.AMANDAKISERART.COM

DEDICATION

Dedicated to my parents who always let me paint and draw on everything and anything.

And to Jesus, Yeshua for saving my life.

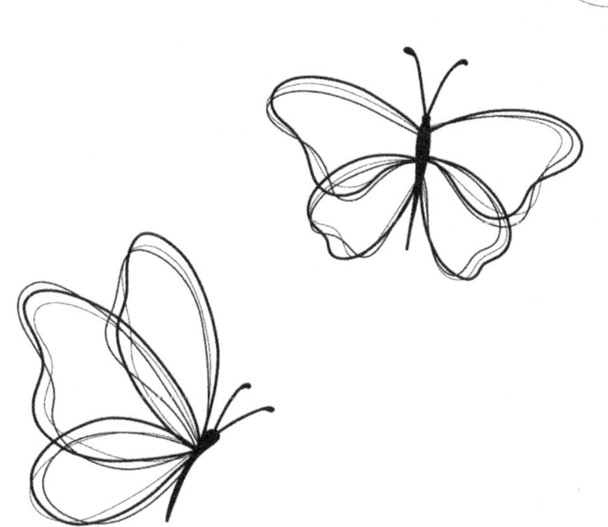

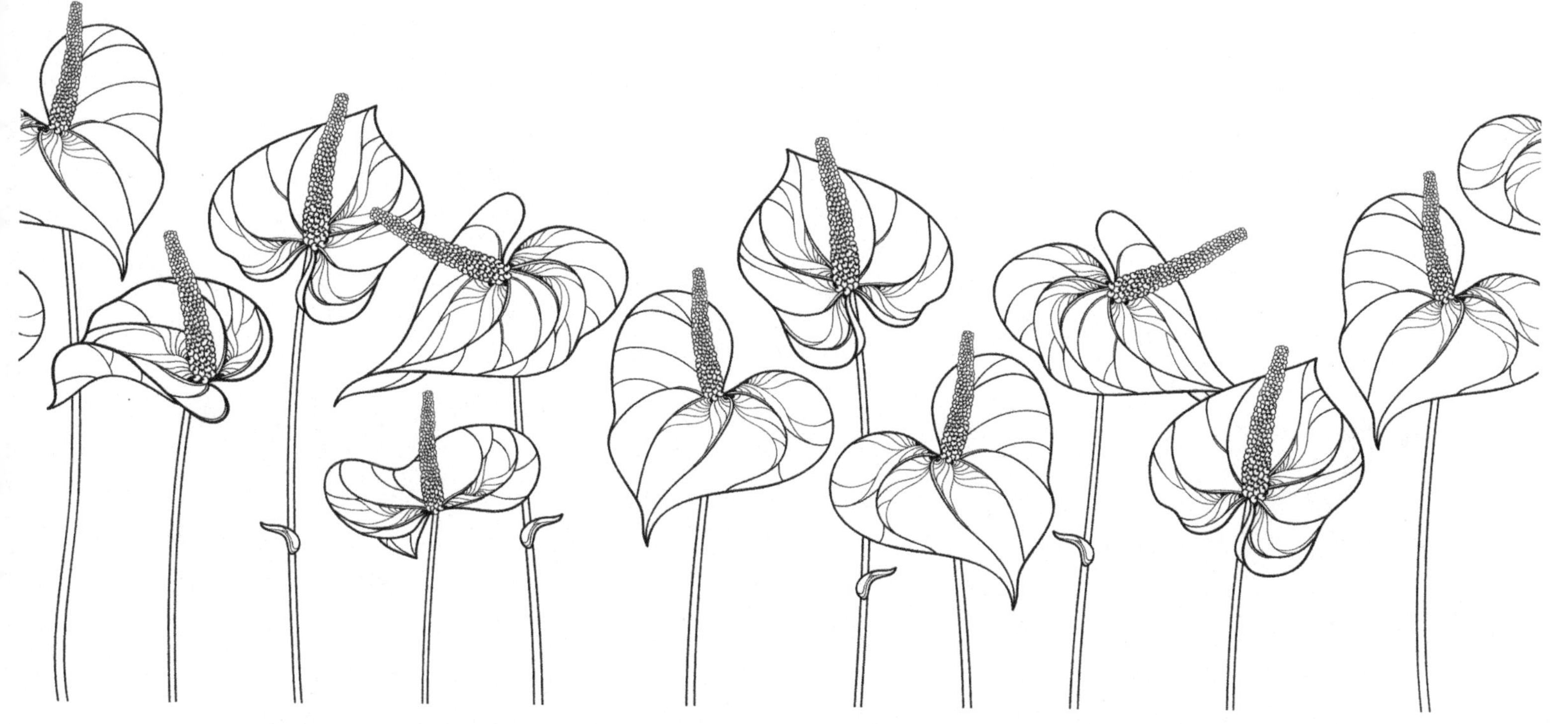

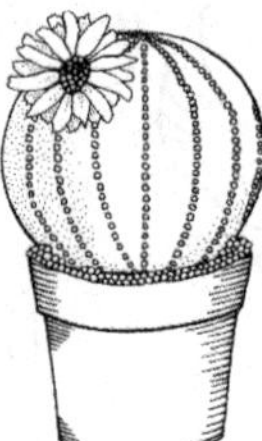

PHILIPPIANS

Track your progress as you color through the scriptures

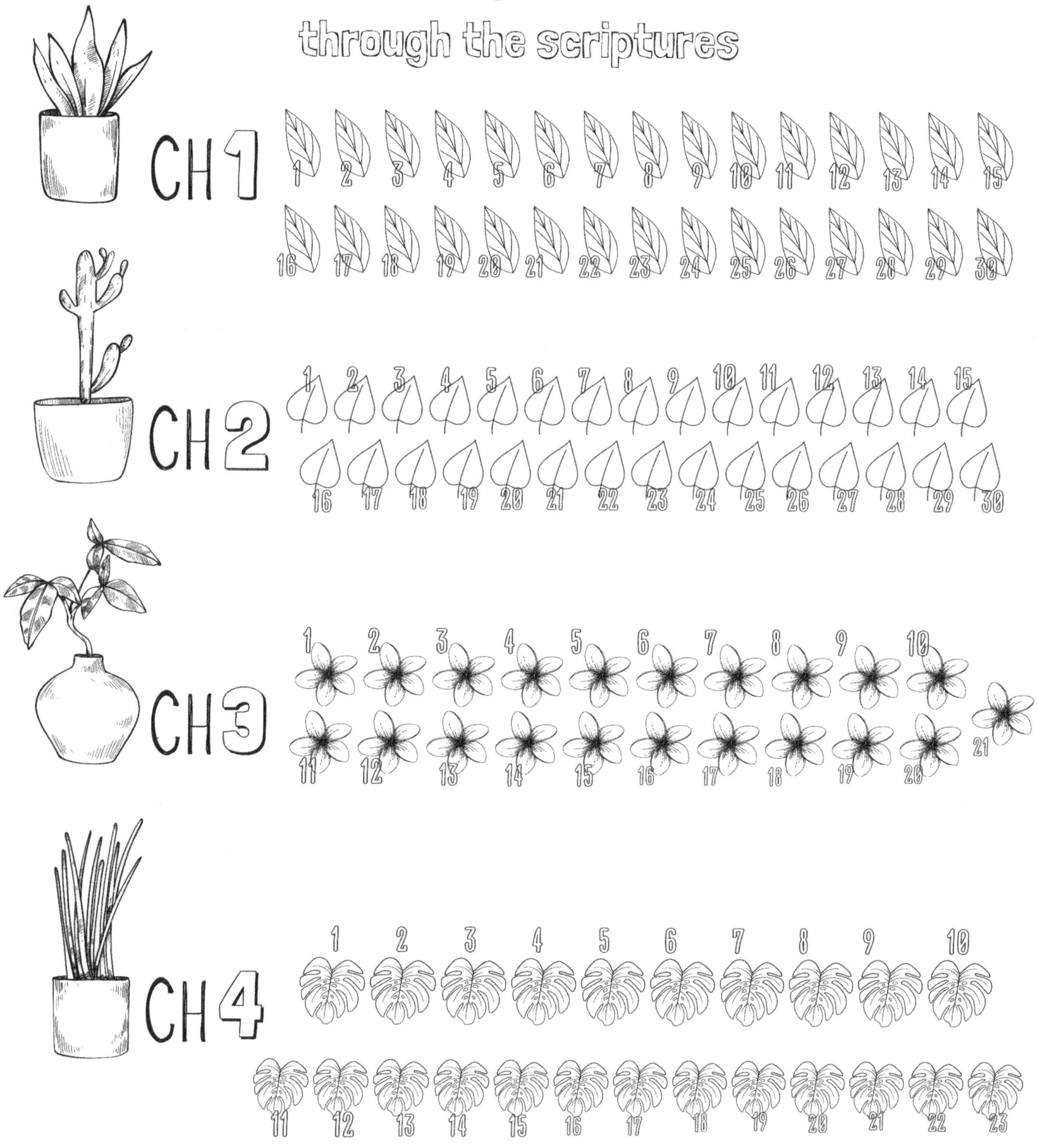

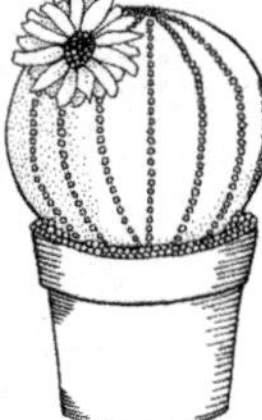

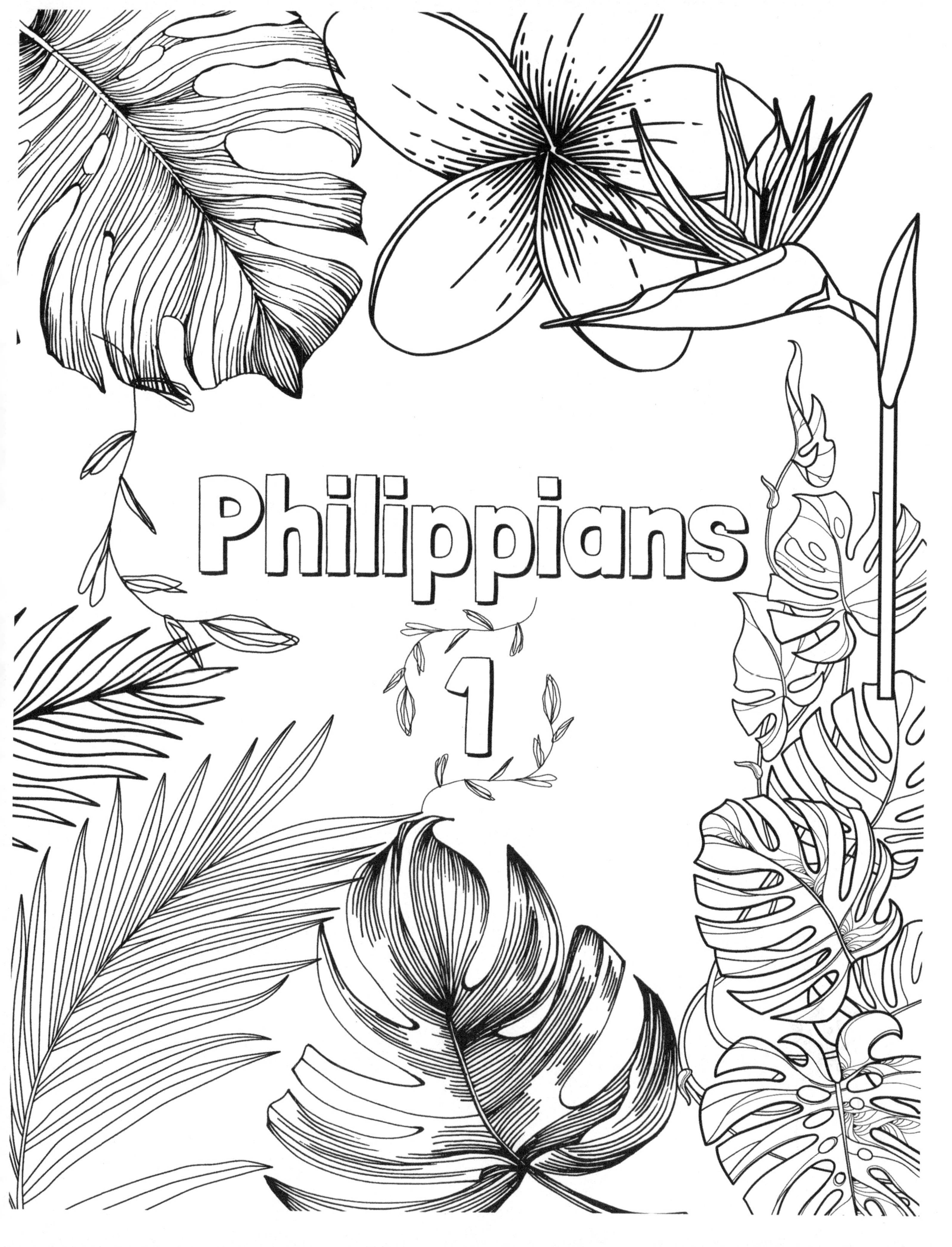
Philippians
1

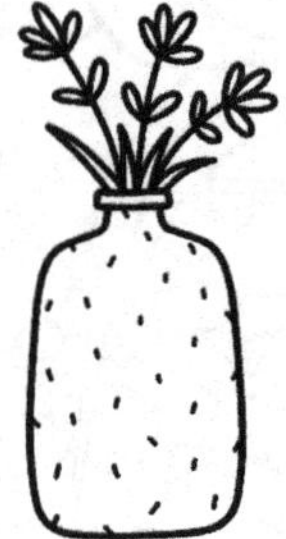

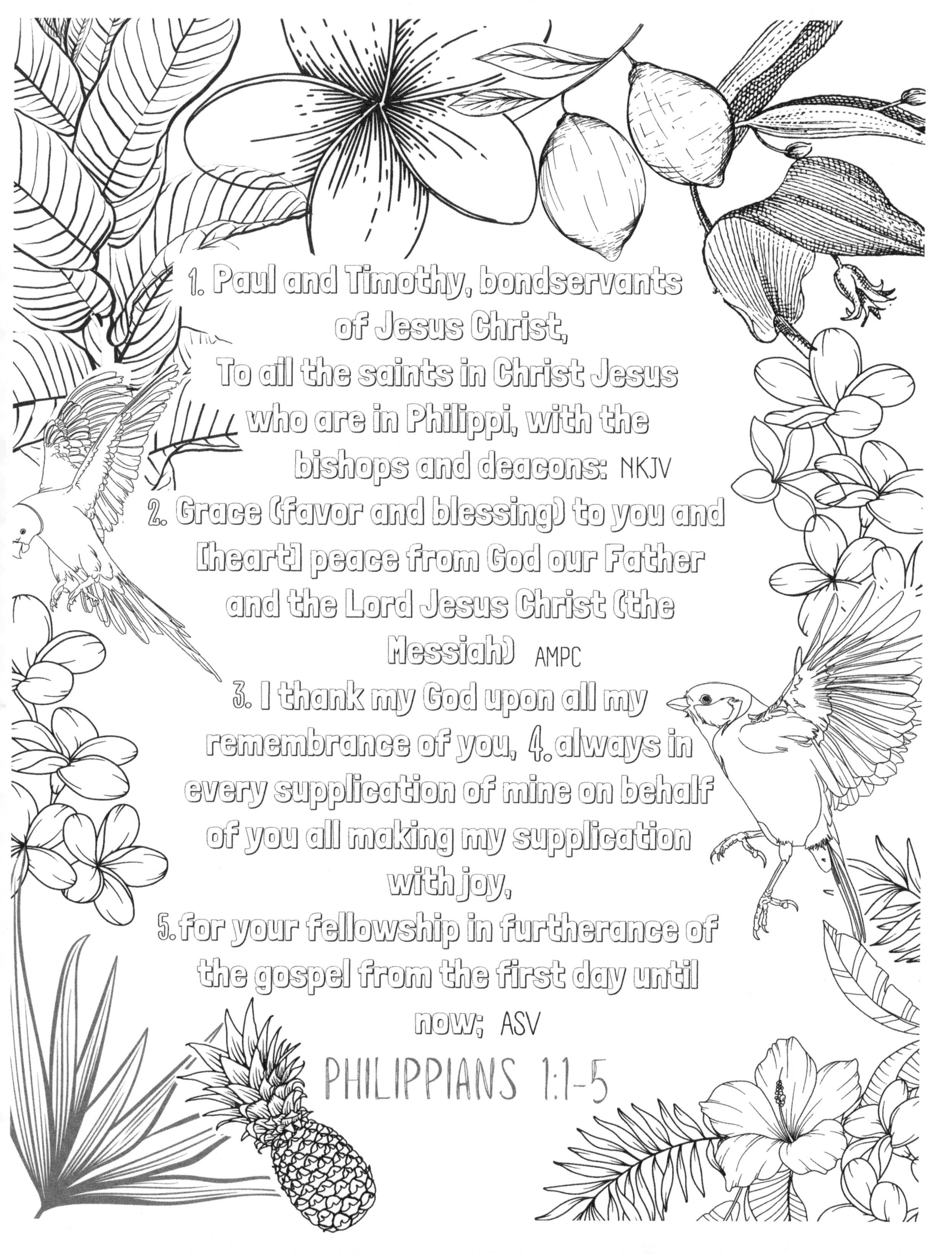
1. Paul and Timothy, bondservants
of Jesus Christ,
To all the saints in Christ Jesus
who are in Philippi, with the
bishops and deacons: NKJV
2. Grace (favor and blessing) to you and
[heart] peace from God our Father
and the Lord Jesus Christ (the
Messiah) AMPC
3. I thank my God upon all my
remembrance of you, 4. always in
every supplication of mine on behalf
of you all making my supplication
with joy,
5. for your fellowship in furtherance of
the gospel from the first day until
now; ASV
PHILIPPIANS 1:1-5

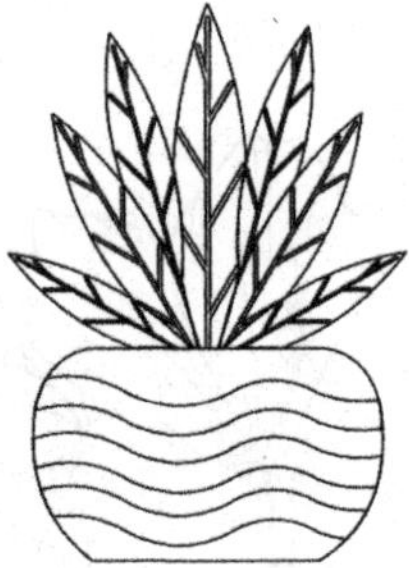

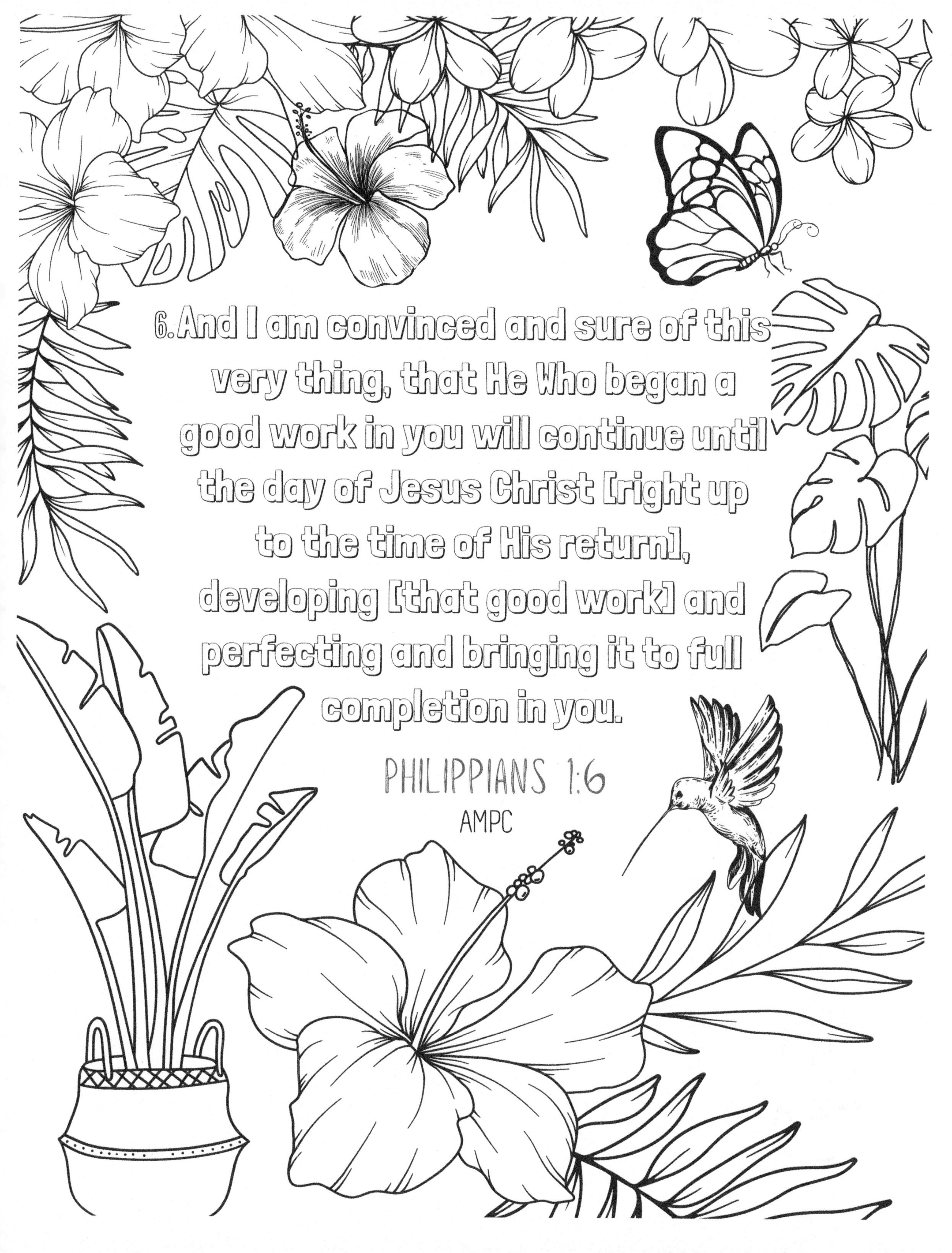
6. And I am convinced and sure of this
very thing, that He Who began a
good work in you will continue until
the day of Jesus Christ [right up
to the time of His return],
developing [that good work] and
perfecting and bringing it to full
completion in you.
PHILIPPIANS 1:6
AMPC

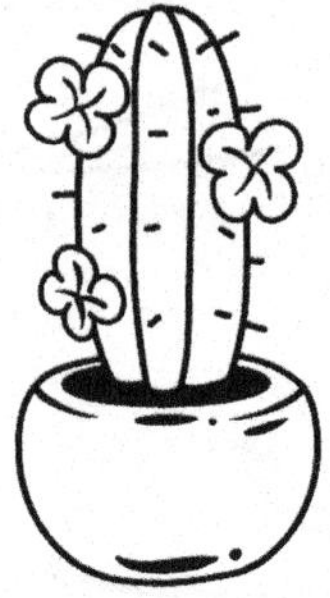

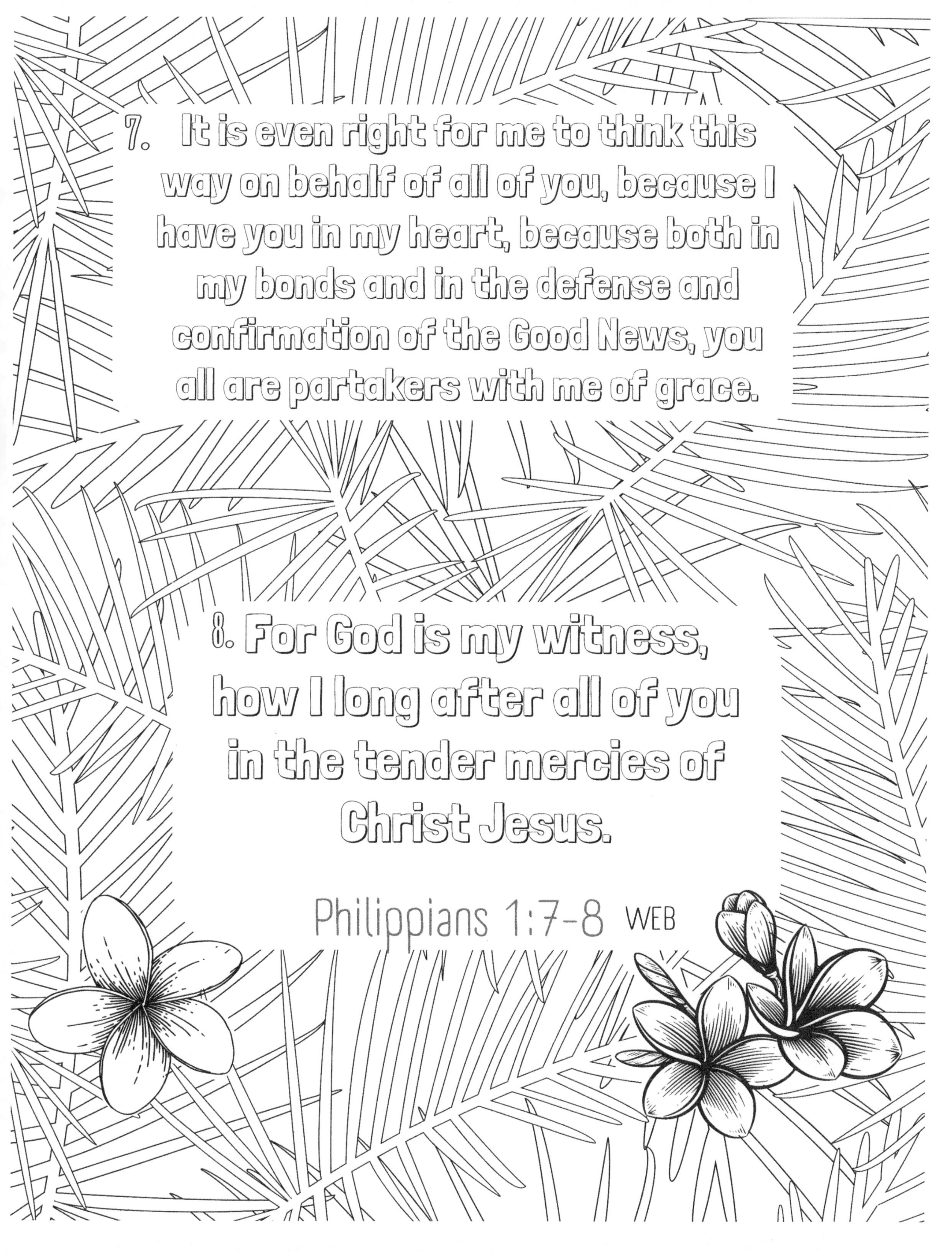
7. It is even right for me to think this
way on behalf of all of you, because I
have you in my heart, because both in
my bonds and in the defense and
confirmation of the Good News, you
all are partakers with me of grace.
8. For God is my witness,
how I long after all of you
in the tender mercies of
Christ Jesus.
Philippians 1:7-8 WEB

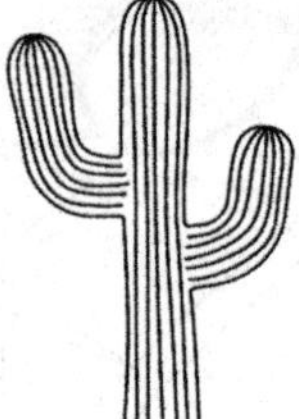

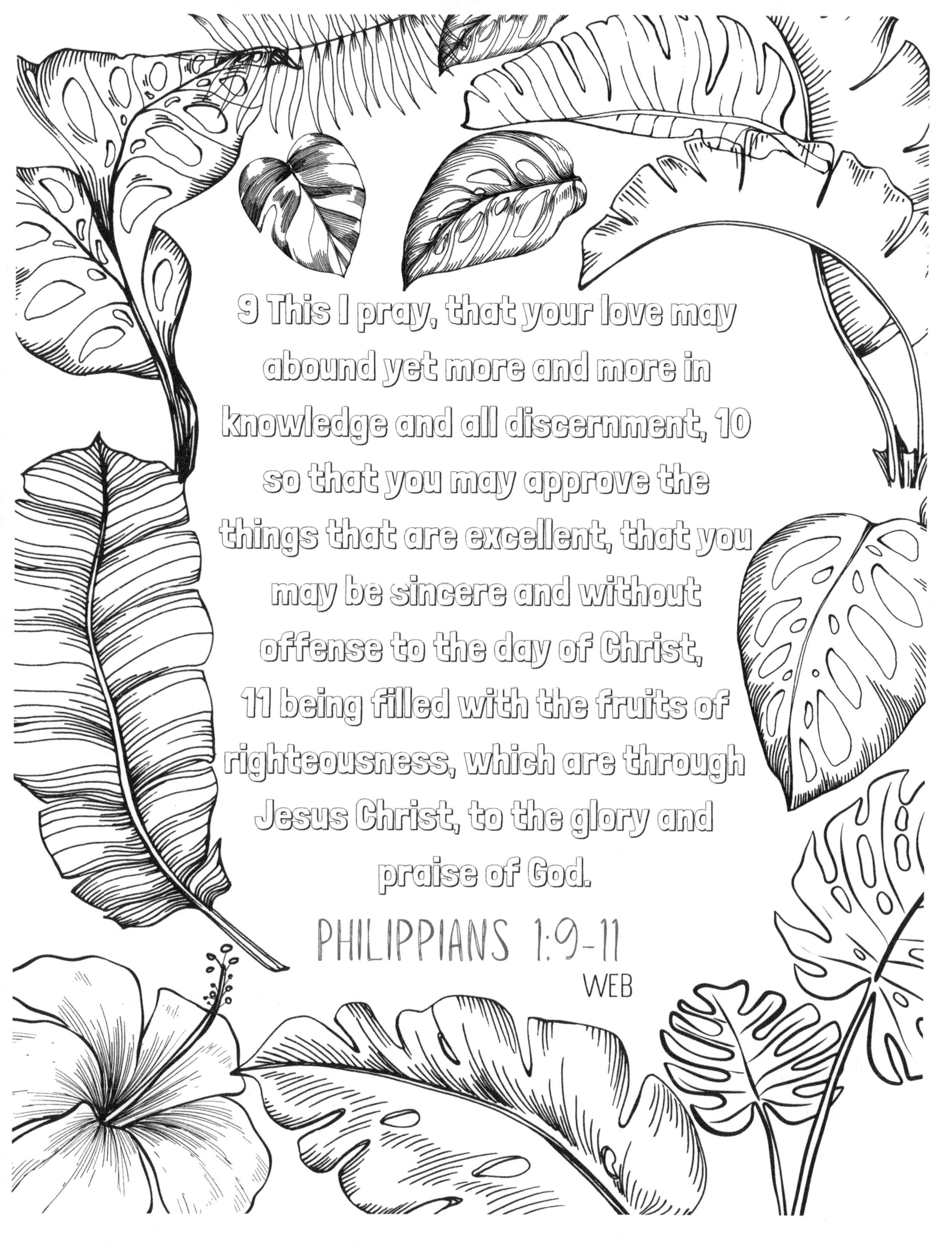
9 This I pray, that your love may
abound yet more and more in
knowledge and all discernment, 10
so that you may approve the
things that are excellent, that you
may be sincere and without
offense to the day of Christ,
11 being filled with the fruits of
righteousness, which are through
Jesus Christ, to the glory and
praise of God.
PHILIPPIANS 1:9-11
WEB

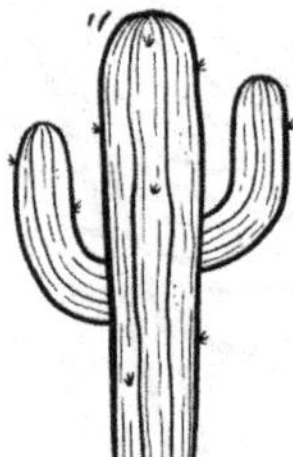

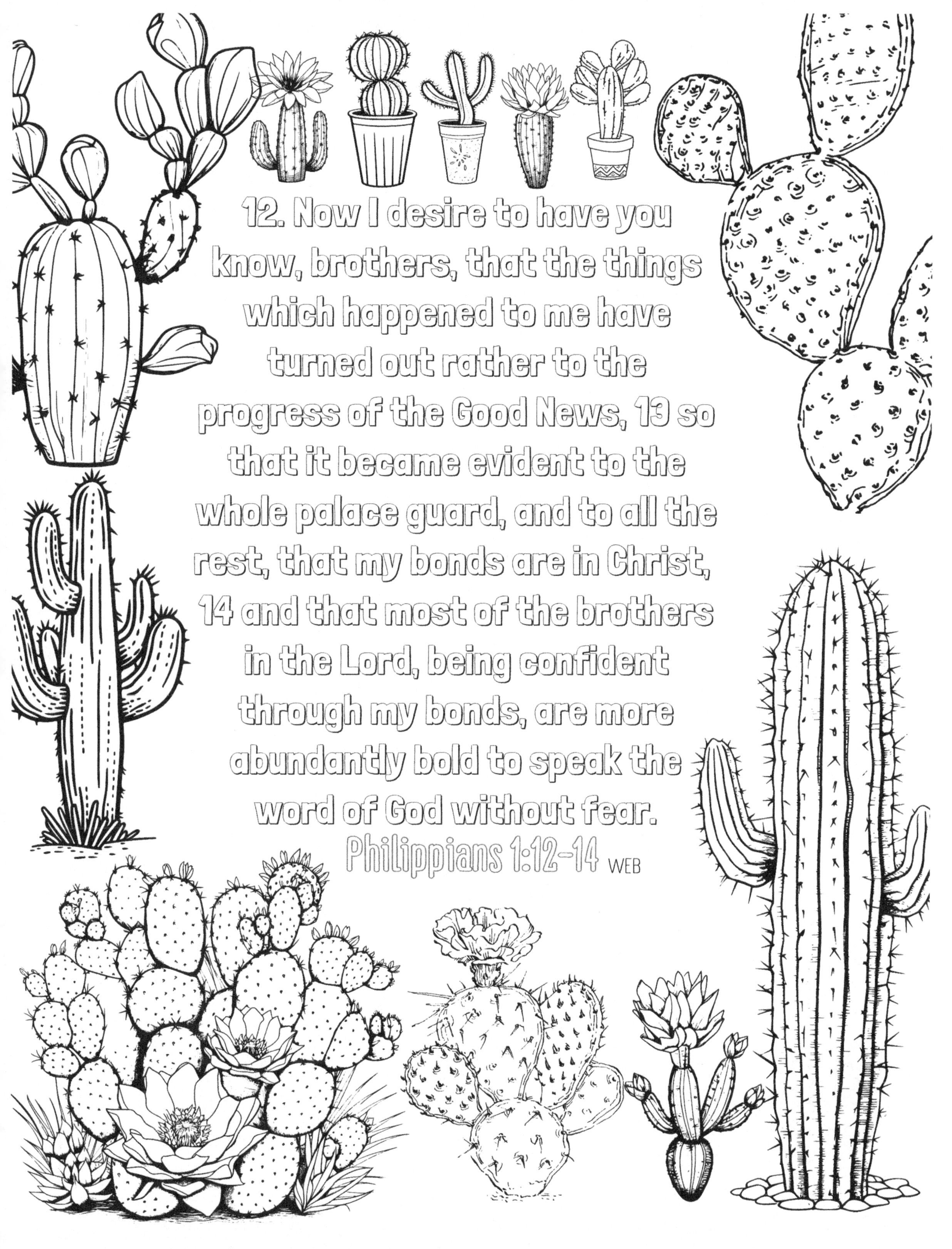
12. Now I desire to have you
know, brothers, that the things
which happened to me have
turned out rather to the
progress of the Good News, 13 so
that it became evident to the
whole palace guard, and to all the
rest, that my bonds are in Christ,
14 and that most of the brothers
in the Lord, being confident
through my bonds, are more
abundantly bold to speak the
word of God without fear.
Philippians 1:12-14 WEB

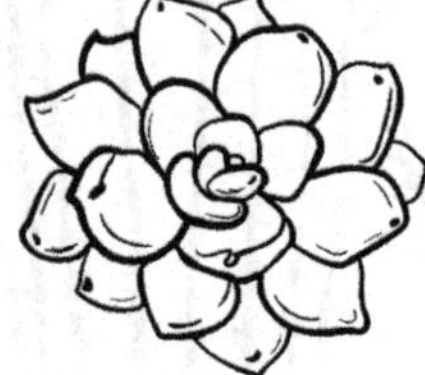

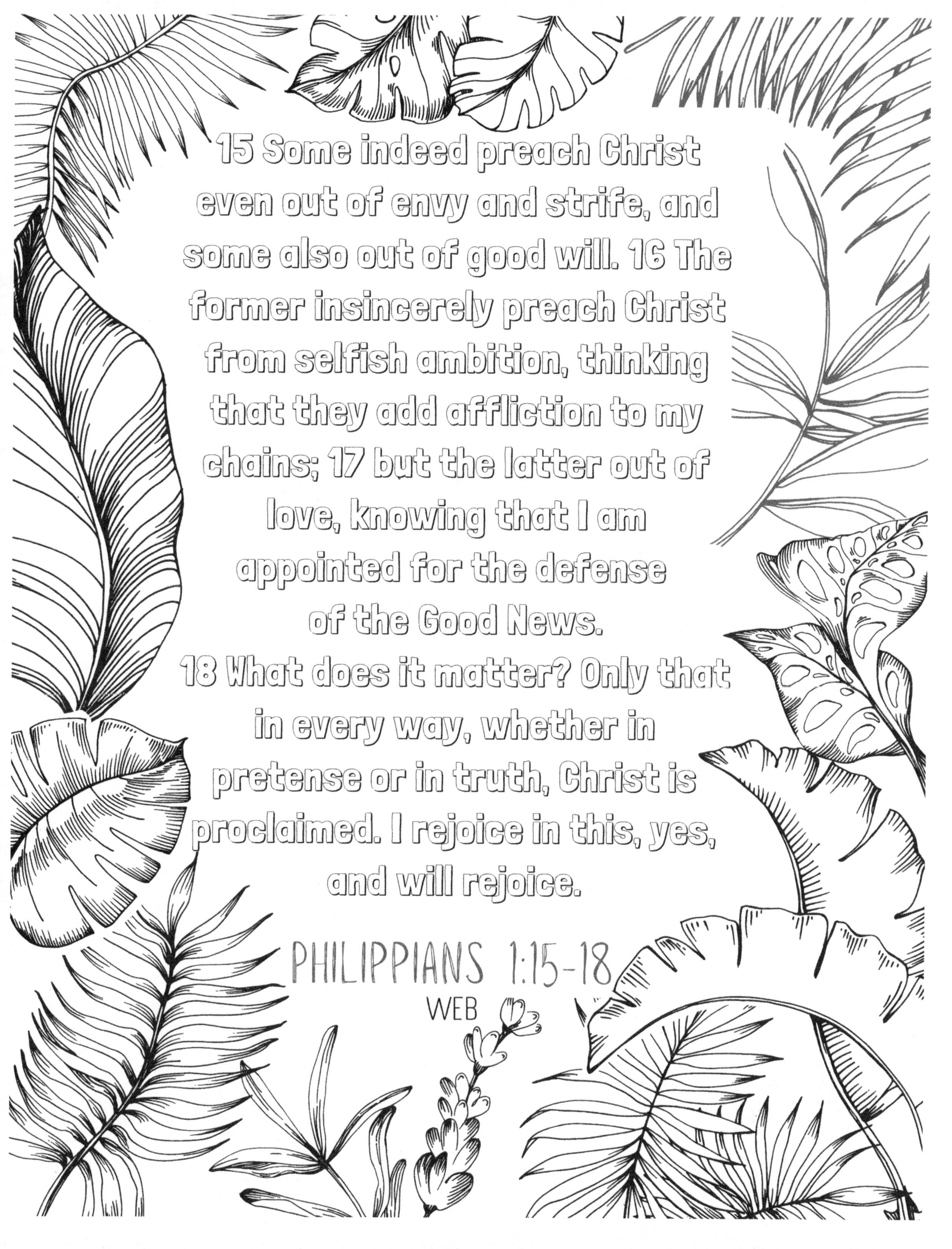
15 Some indeed preach Christ
even out of envy and strife, and
some also out of good will. 16 The
former insincerely preach Christ
from selfish ambition, thinking
that they add affliction to my
chains; 17 but the latter out of
love, knowing that I am
appointed for the defense
of the Good News.
18 What does it matter? Only that
in every way, whether in
pretense or in truth, Christ is
proclaimed. I rejoice in this, yes,
and will rejoice.
PHILIPPIANS 1:15-18
WEB

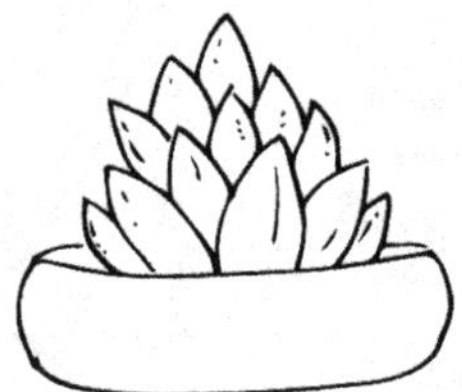

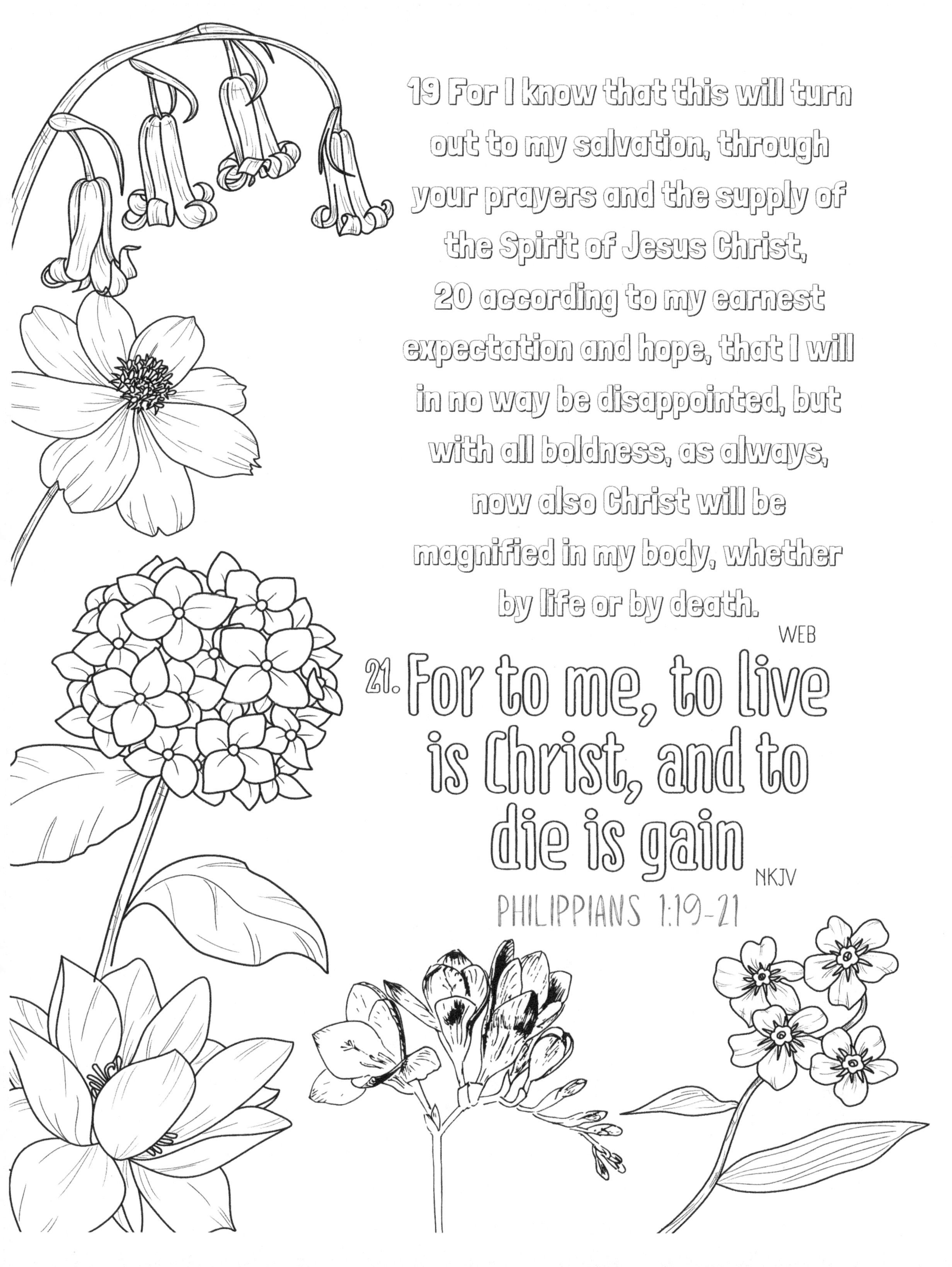
19 For I know that this will turn
out to my salvation, through
your prayers and the supply of
the Spirit of Jesus Christ,
20 according to my earnest
expectation and hope, that I will
in no way be disappointed, but
with all boldness, as always,
now also Christ will be
magnified in my body, whether
by life or by death.
WEB
21. For to me, to live
is Christ, and to
die is gain
NKJV
PHILIPPIANS 1:19-21

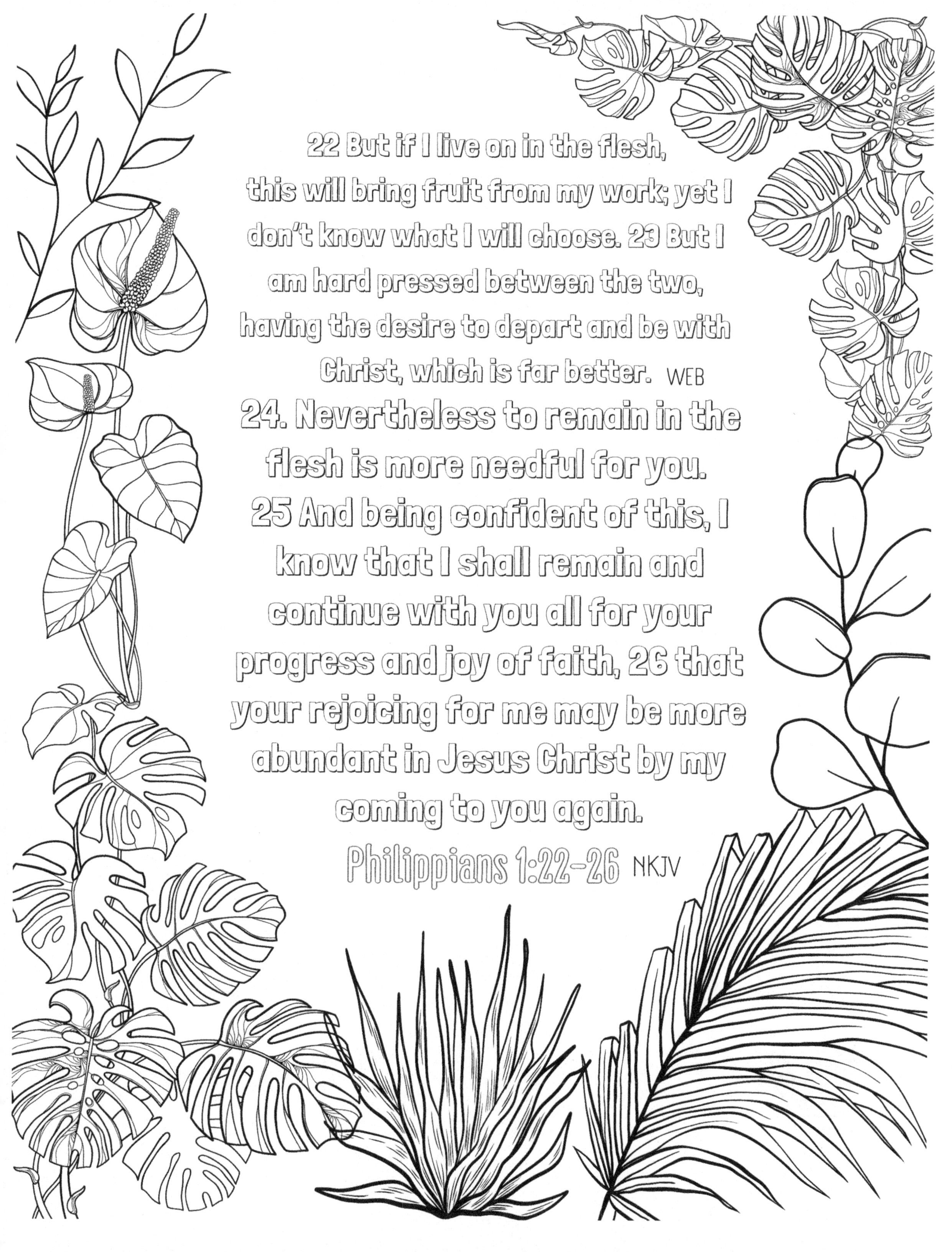
22 But if I live on in the flesh,
this will bring fruit from my work; yet I
don't know what I will choose. 23 But I
am hard pressed between the two,
having the desire to depart and be with
Christ, which is far better. WEB
24. Nevertheless to remain in the
flesh is more needful for you.
25 And being confident of this, I
know that I shall remain and
continue with you all for your
progress and joy of faith, 26 that
your rejoicing for me may be more
abundant in Jesus Christ by my
coming to you again.
Philippians 1:22-26 NKJV

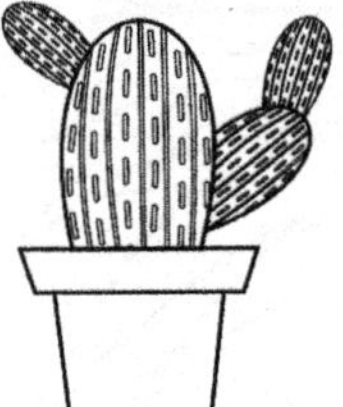

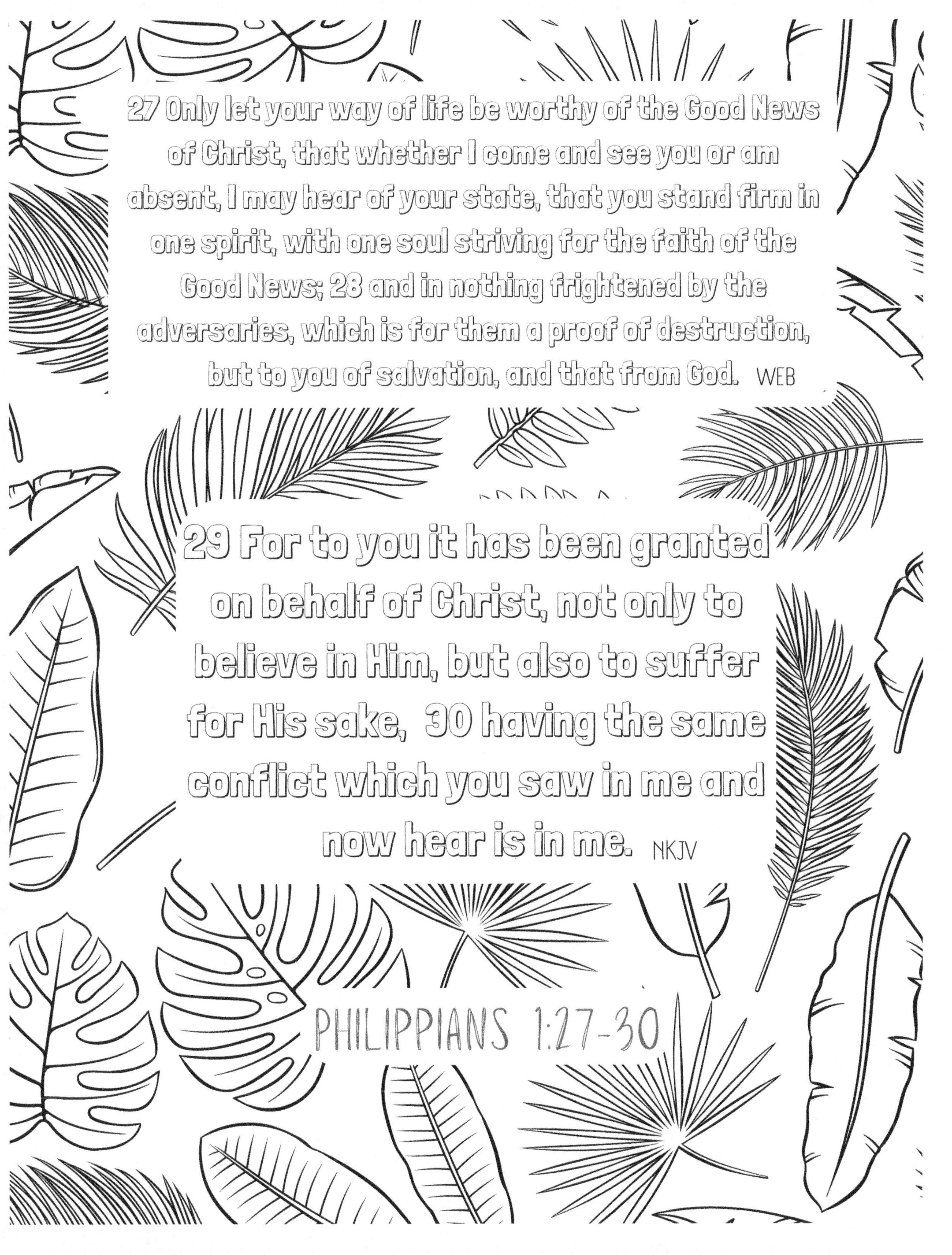
27 Only let your way of life be worthy of the Good News
of Christ, that whether I come and see you or am
absent, I may hear of your state, that you stand firm in
one spirit, with one soul striving for the faith of the
Good News; 28 and in nothing frightened by the
adversaries, which is for them a proof of destruction,
but to you of salvation, and that from God. WEB
29 For to you it has been granted
on behalf of Christ, not only to
believe in Him, but also to suffer
for His sake, 30 having the same
conflict which you saw in me and
now hear is in me. NKJV
PHILIPPIANS 1:27-30

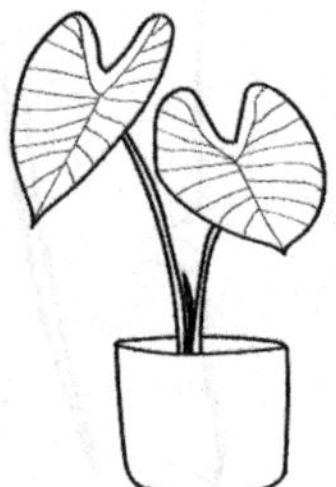

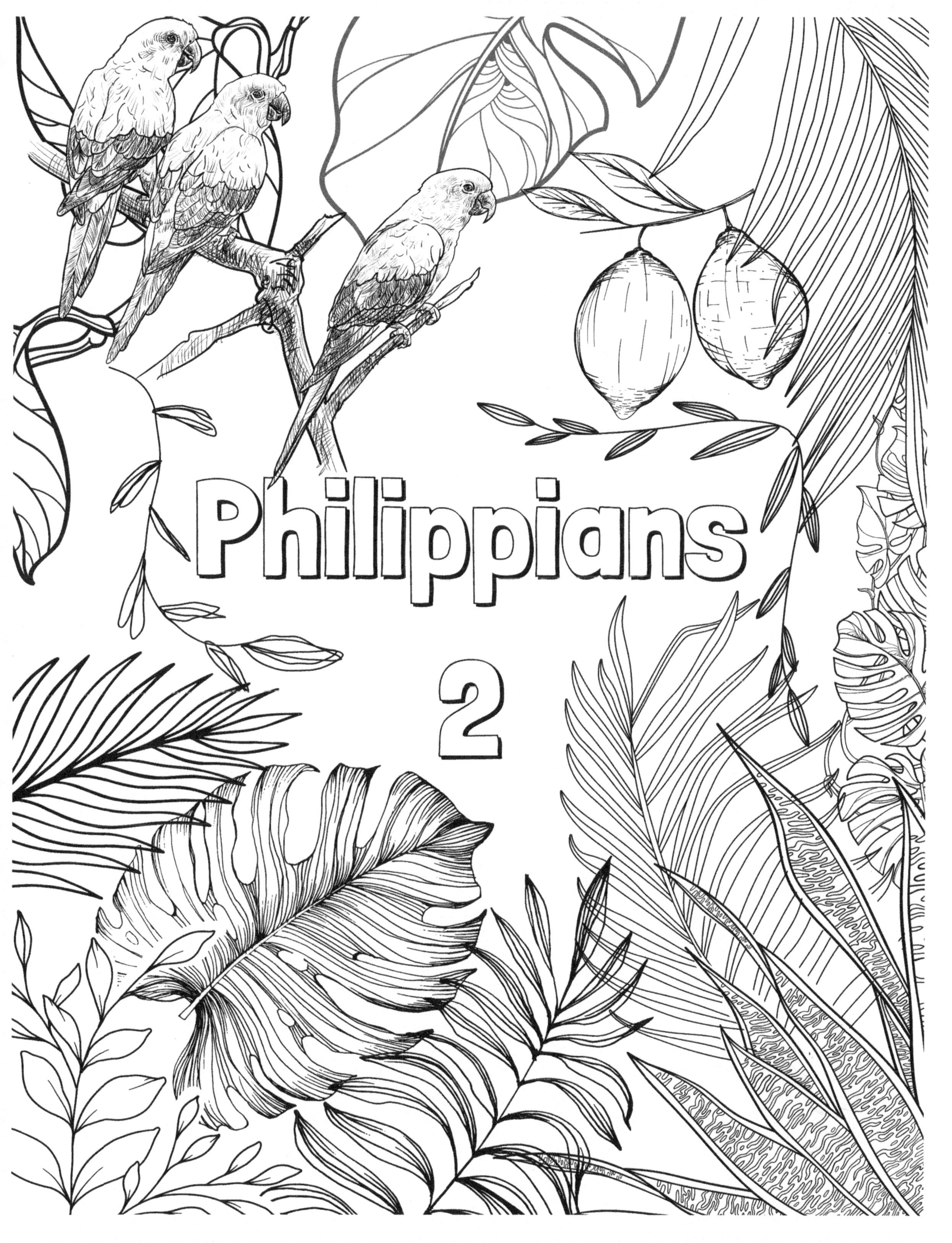
Philippians
2

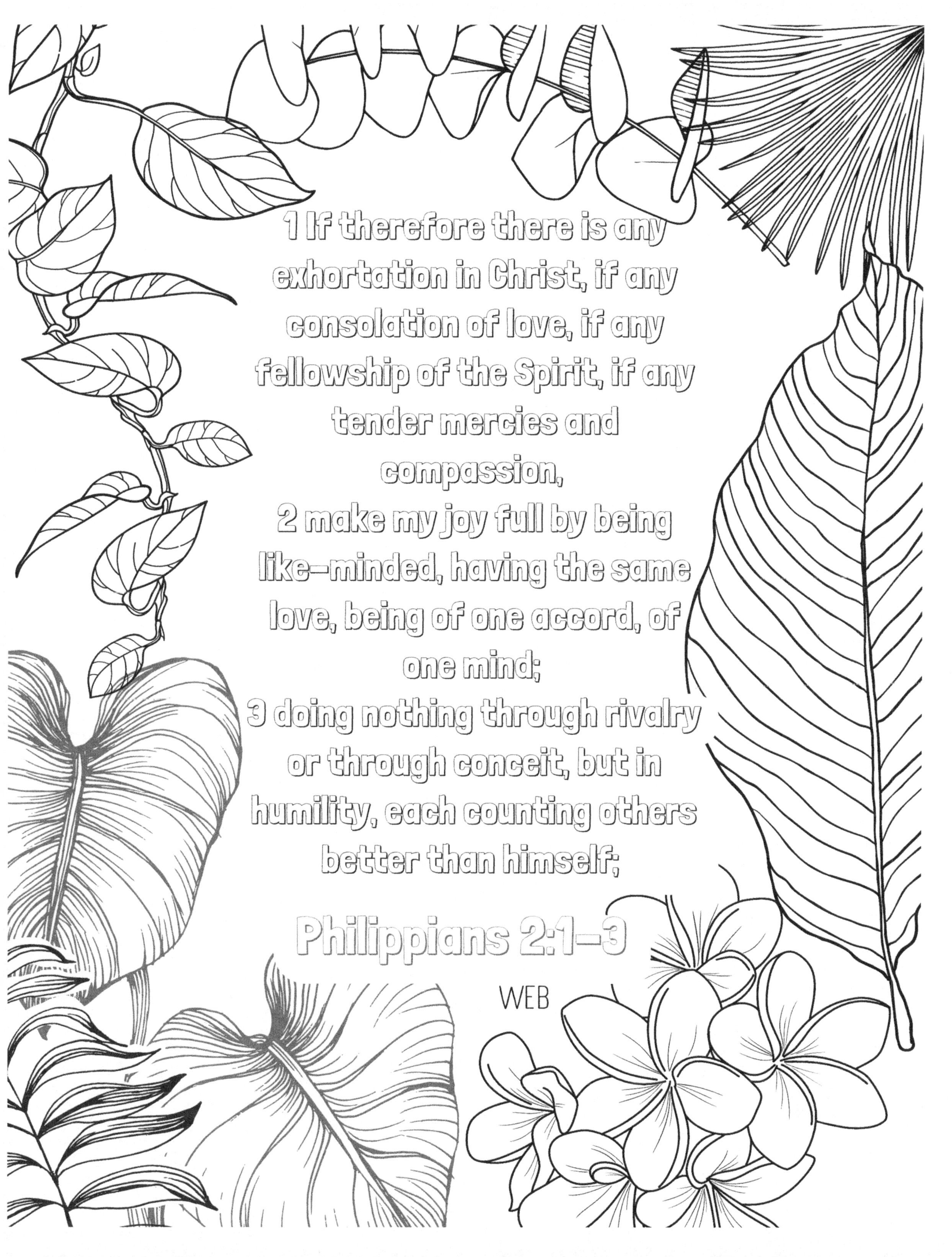
1 If therefore there is any
exhortation in Christ, if any
consolation of love, if any
fellowship of the Spirit, if any
tender mercies and
compassion,
2 make my joy full by being
like-minded, having the same
love, being of one accord, of
one mind;
3 doing nothing through rivalry
or through conceit, but in
humility, each counting others
better than himself;
Philippians 2:1-3
WEB

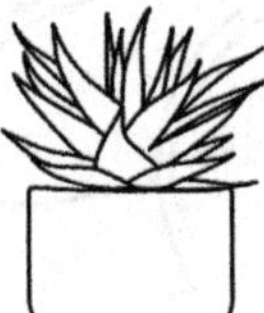

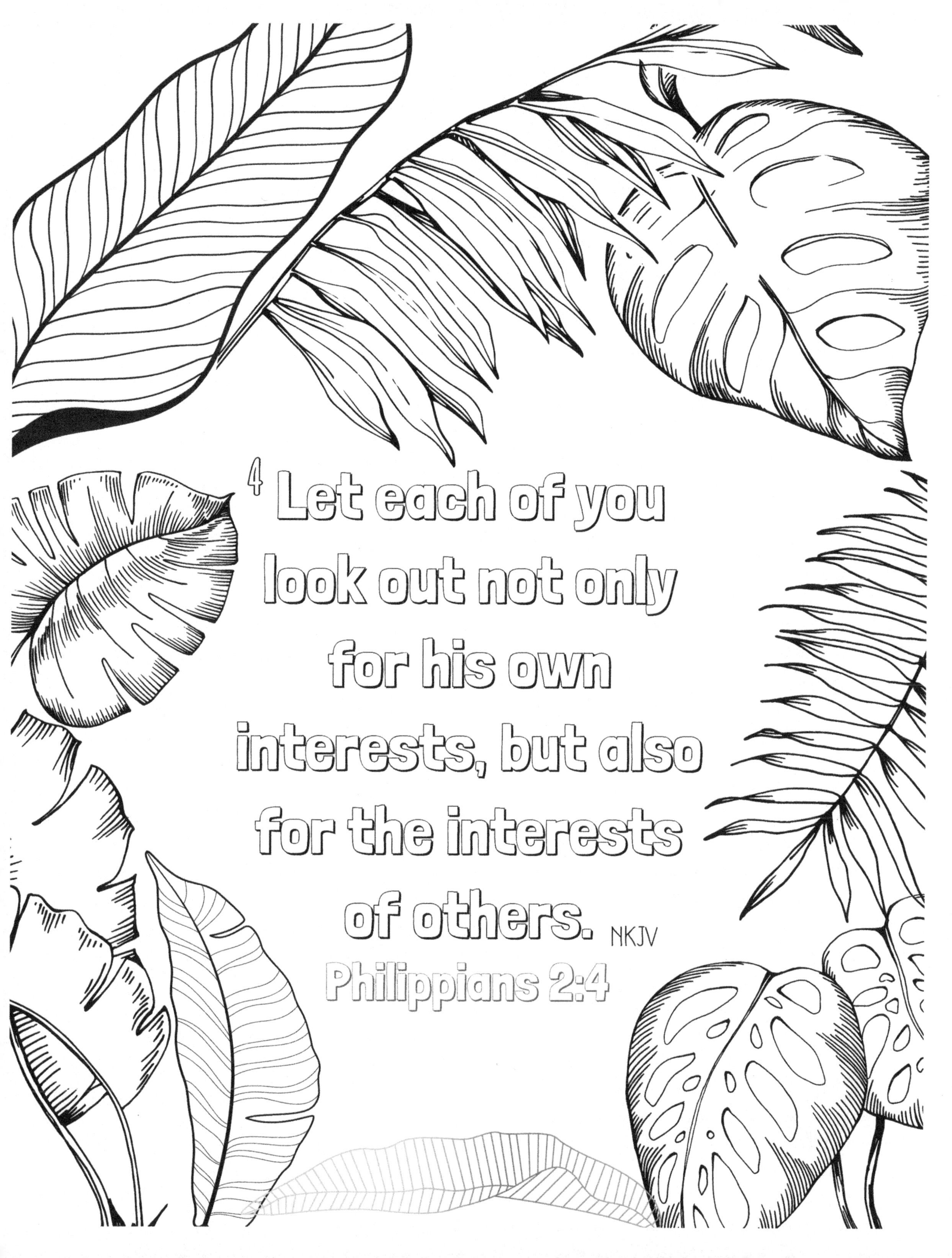
4 Let each of you
look out not only
for his own
interests, but also
for the interests
of others. NKJV
Philippians 2:4

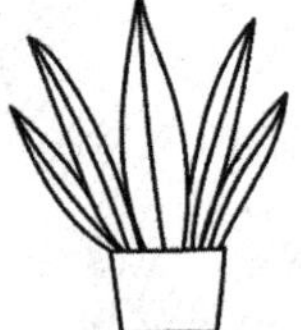

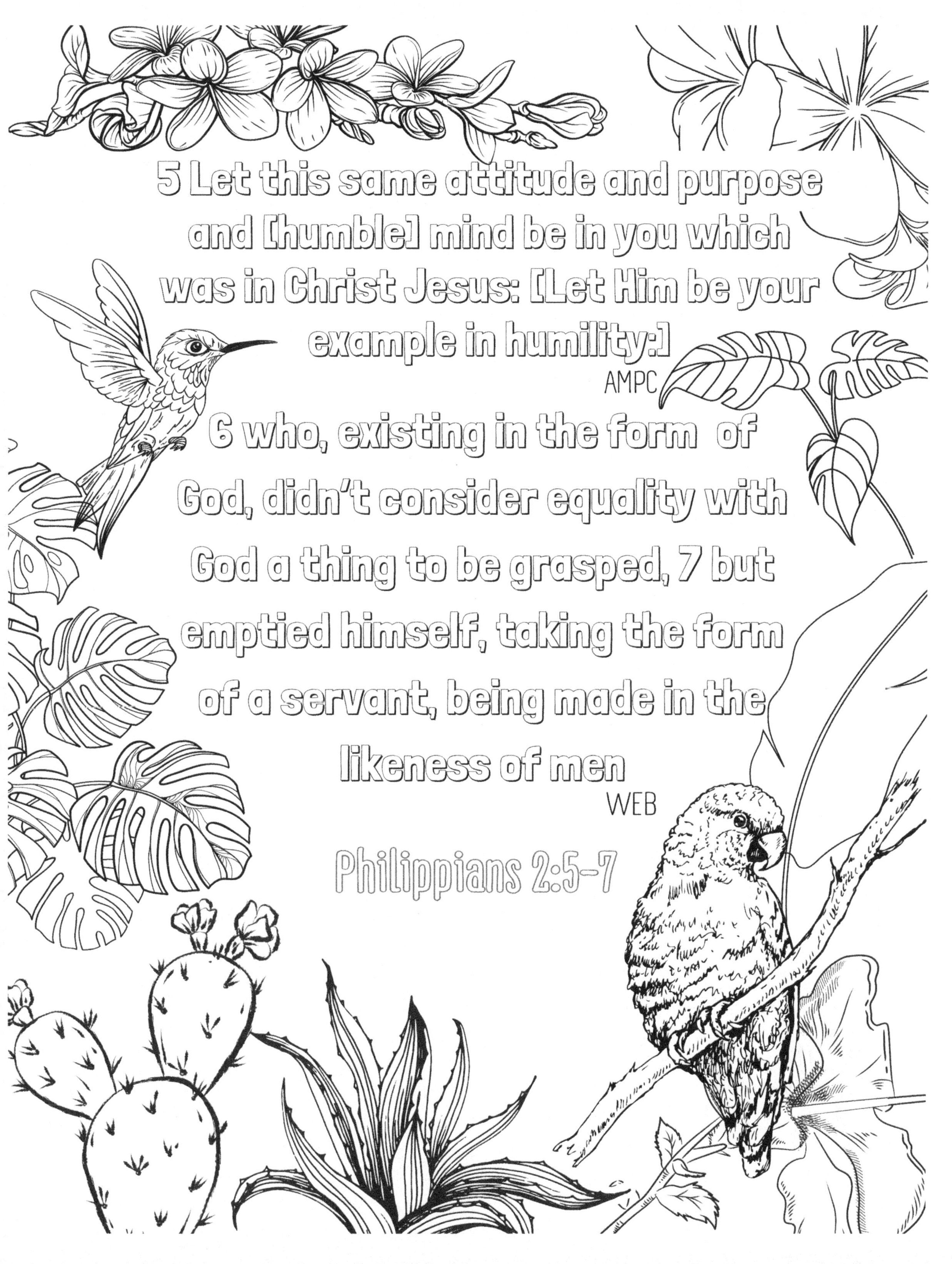
5 Let this same attitude and purpose
and [humble] mind be in you which
was in Christ Jesus: [Let Him be your
example in humility:]
AMPC
6 who, existing in the form of
God, didn't consider equality with
God a thing to be grasped, 7 but
emptied himself, taking the form
of a servant, being made in the
likeness of men
WEB
Philippians 2:5-7

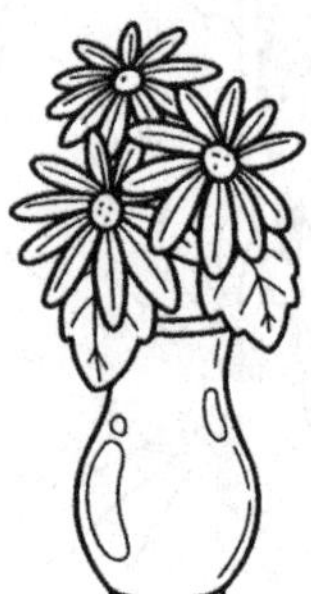

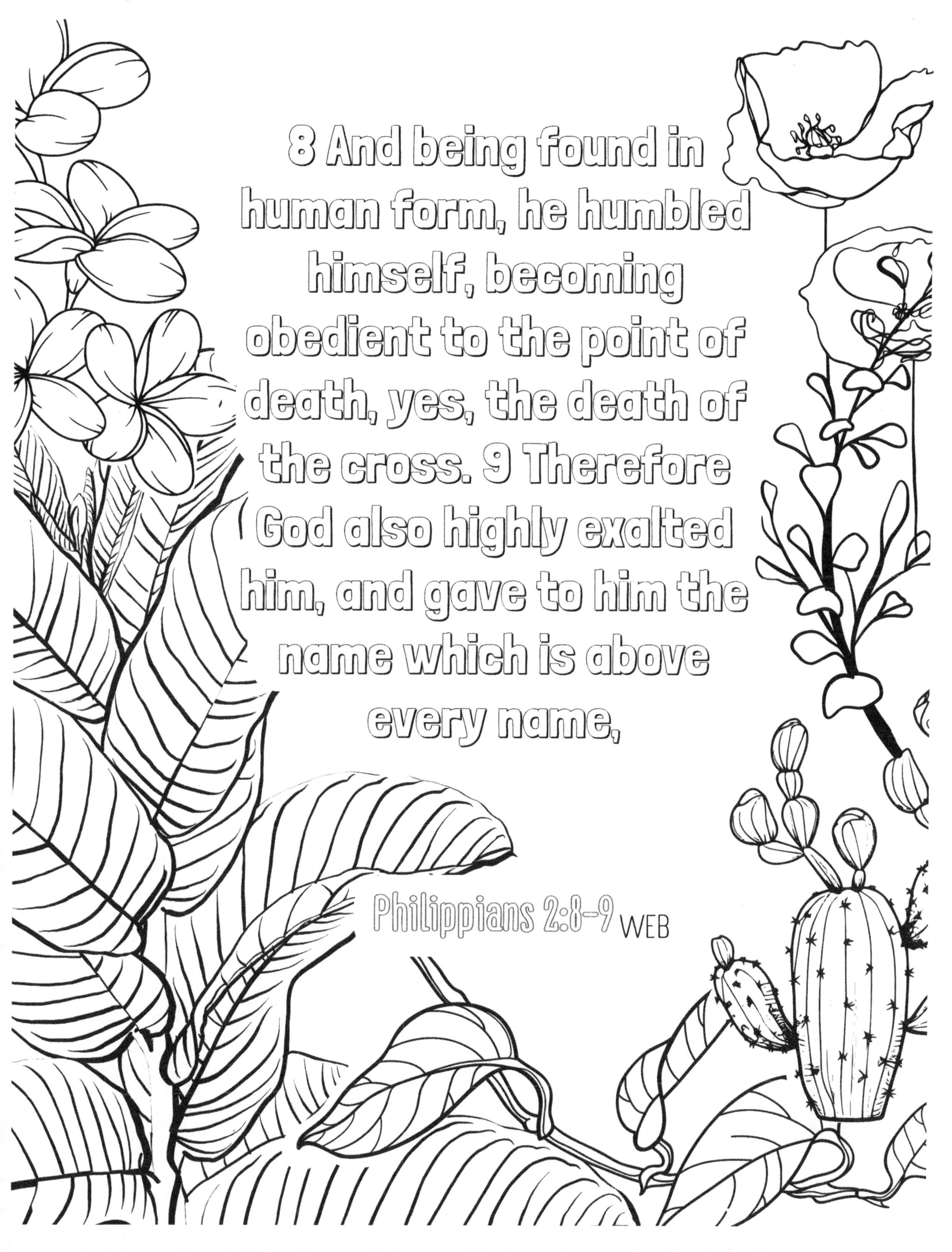
8 And being found in
human form, he humbled
himself, becoming
obedient to the point of
death, yes, the death of
the cross. 9 Therefore
God also highly exalted
him, and gave to him the
name which is above
every name,
Philippians 2:8-9 WEB

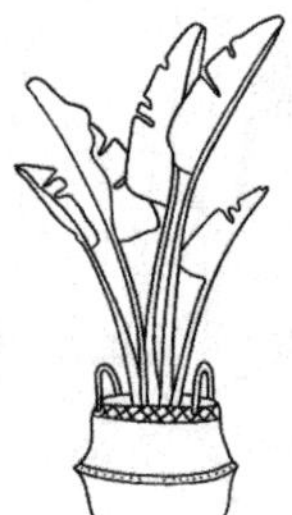

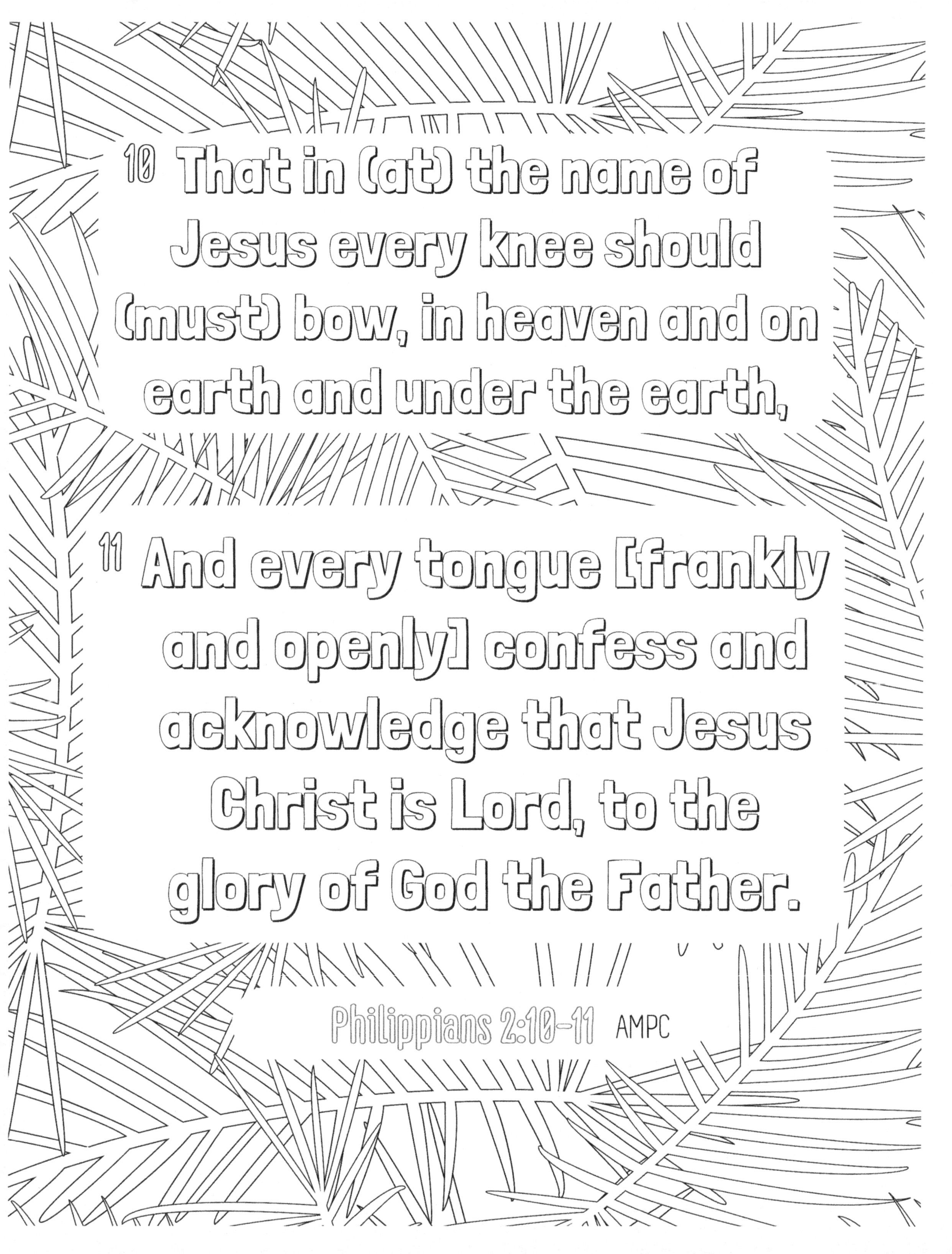
10 That in (at) the name of
Jesus every knee should
(must) bow, in heaven and on
earth and under the earth,
11 And every tongue [frankly
and openly] confess and
acknowledge that Jesus
Christ is Lord, to the
glory of God the Father.
Philippians 2:10-11 AMPC

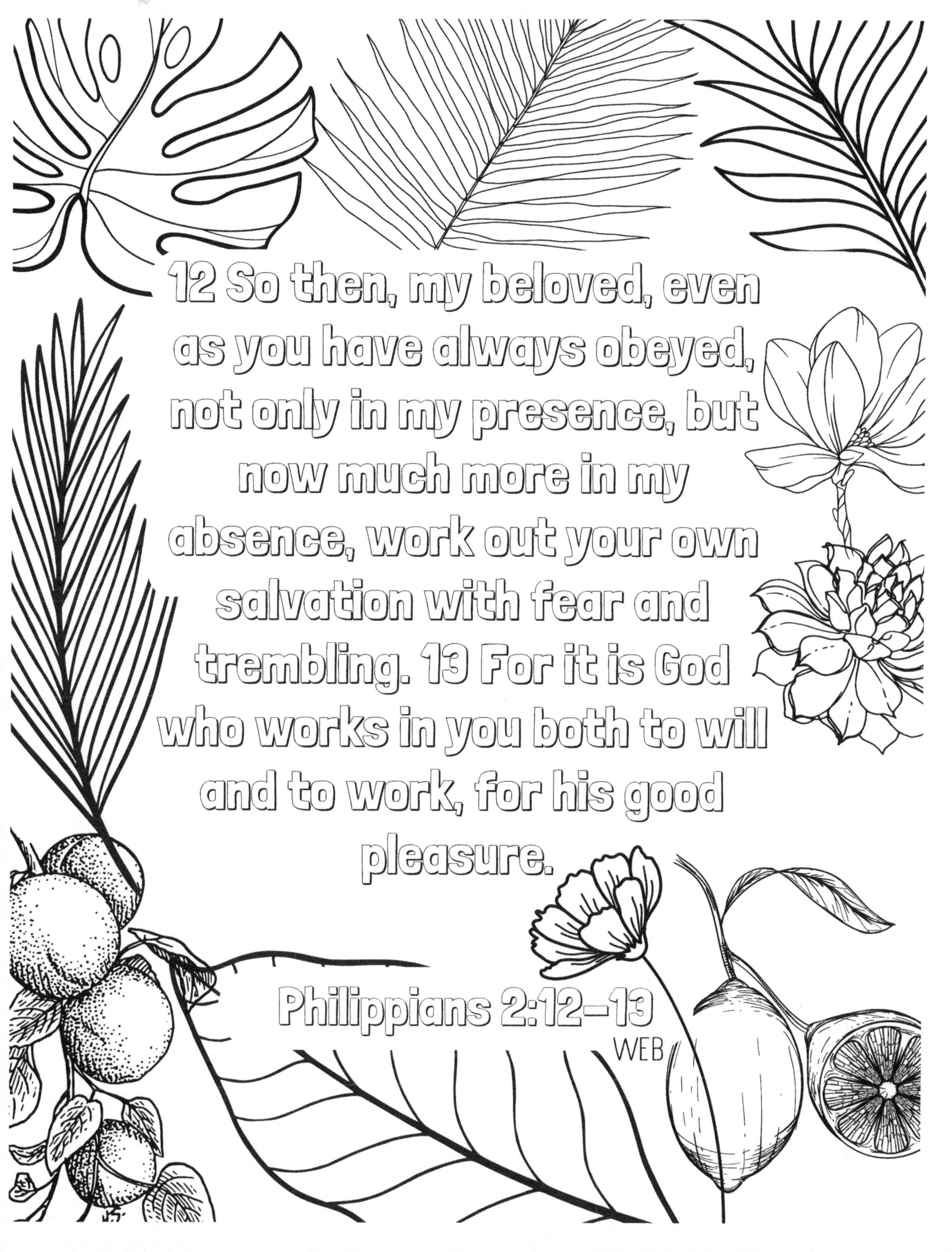
12 So then, my beloved, even
as you have always obeyed,
not only in my presence, but
now much more in my
absence, work out your own
salvation with fear and
trembling. 13 For it is God
who works in you both to will
and to work, for his good
pleasure.
Philippians 2:12-13
WEB

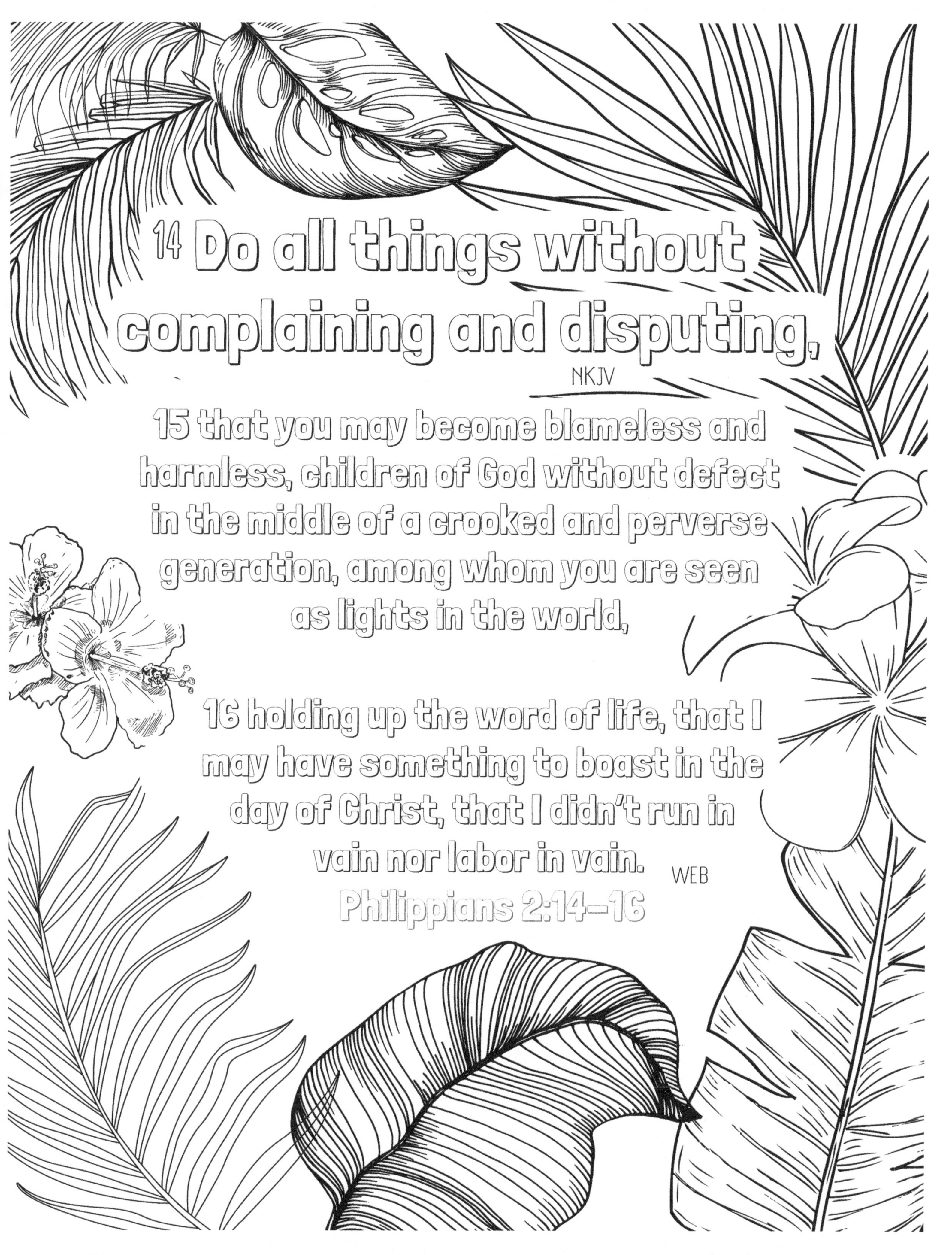
14 Do all things without
complaining and disputing,
NKJV
15 that you may become blameless and
harmless, children of God without defect
in the middle of a crooked and perverse
generation, among whom you are seen
as lights in the world,
16 holding up the word of life, that I
may have something to boast in the
day of Christ, that I didn't run in
vain nor labor in vain.
WEB
Philippians 2:14–16

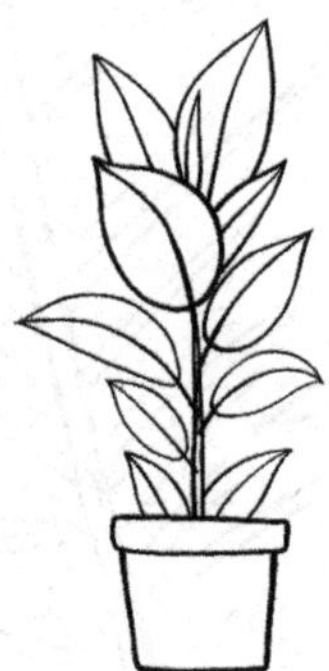

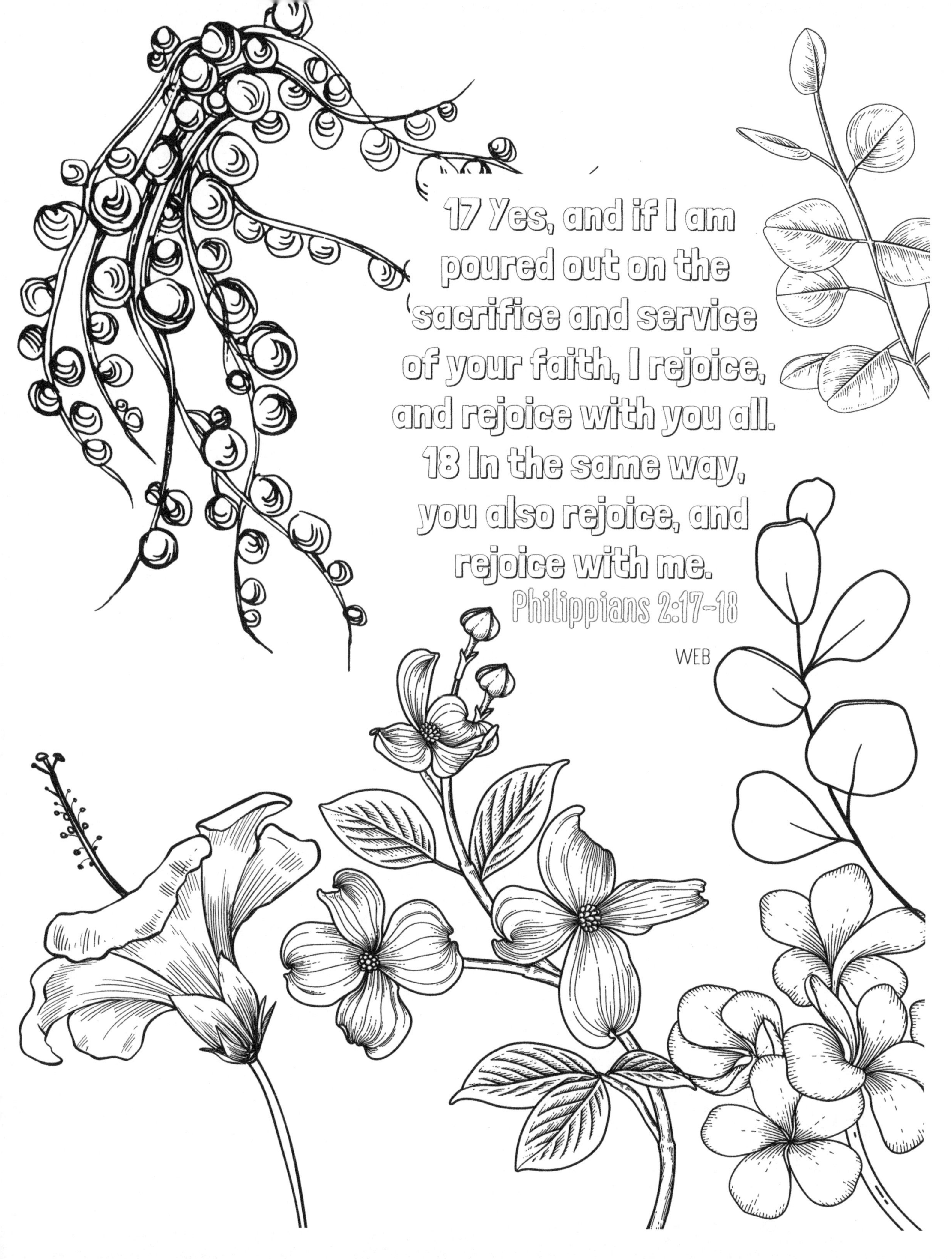
17 Yes, and if I am
poured out on the
sacrifice and service
of your faith, I rejoice,
and rejoice with you all.
18 In the same way,
you also rejoice, and
rejoice with me.
Philippians 2:17-18
WEB

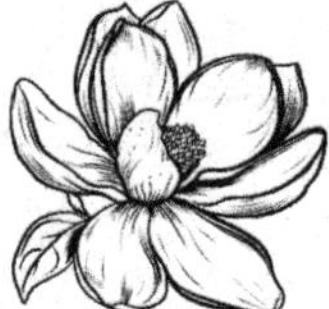

19 But I hope in the Lord Jesus
to send Timothy to you soon,
that I also may be cheered up
when I know how you are
doing.
20 For I have no one else like-
minded, who will truly care
about you. 21 For they all seek
their own, not the things of
Jesus Christ.
22 But you know the proof of
him, that as a child serves a
father, so he served with me
in furtherance of the Good
News.
23 Therefore I hope to send
him at once, as soon as I see
how it will go with me.
24 But I trust in the Lord that
I myself also will come
shortly.

Philippians 2:19-24

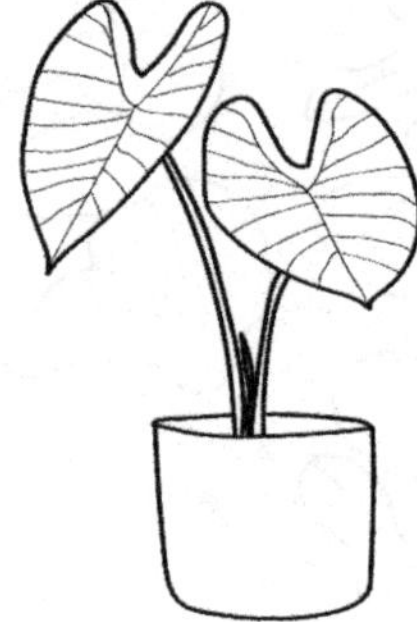

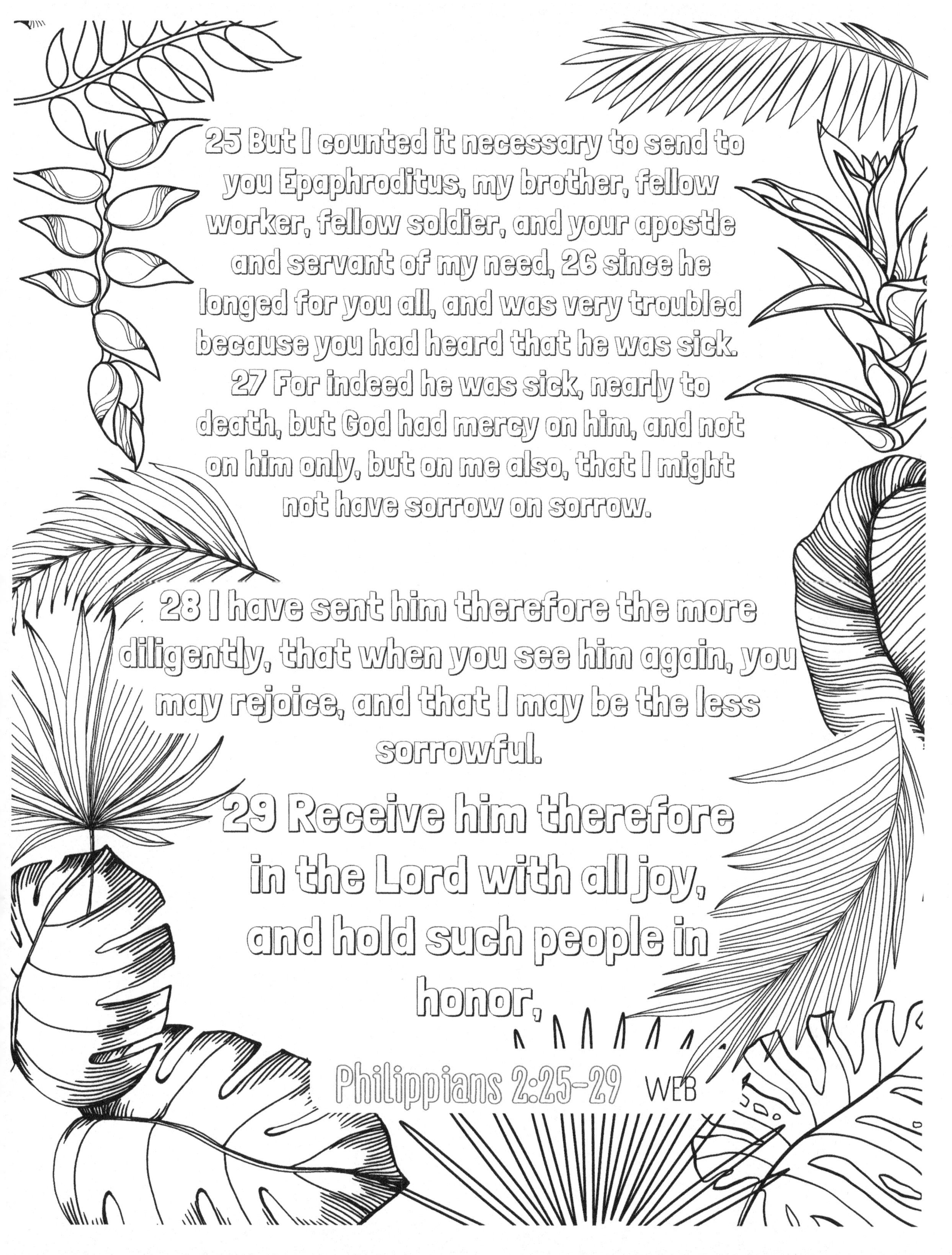
25 But I counted it necessary to send to
you Epaphroditus, my brother, fellow
worker, fellow soldier, and your apostle
and servant of my need, 26 since he
longed for you all, and was very troubled
because you had heard that he was sick.
27 For indeed he was sick, nearly to
death, but God had mercy on him, and not
on him only, but on me also, that I might
not have sorrow on sorrow.
28 I have sent him therefore the more
diligently, that when you see him again, you
may rejoice, and that I may be the less
sorrowful.
29 Receive him therefore
in the Lord with all joy,
and hold such people in
honor,
Philippians 2:25-29 WEB

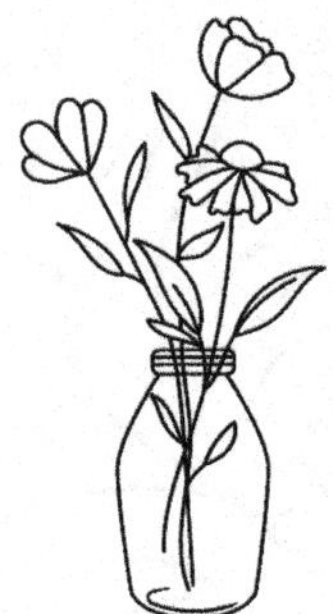

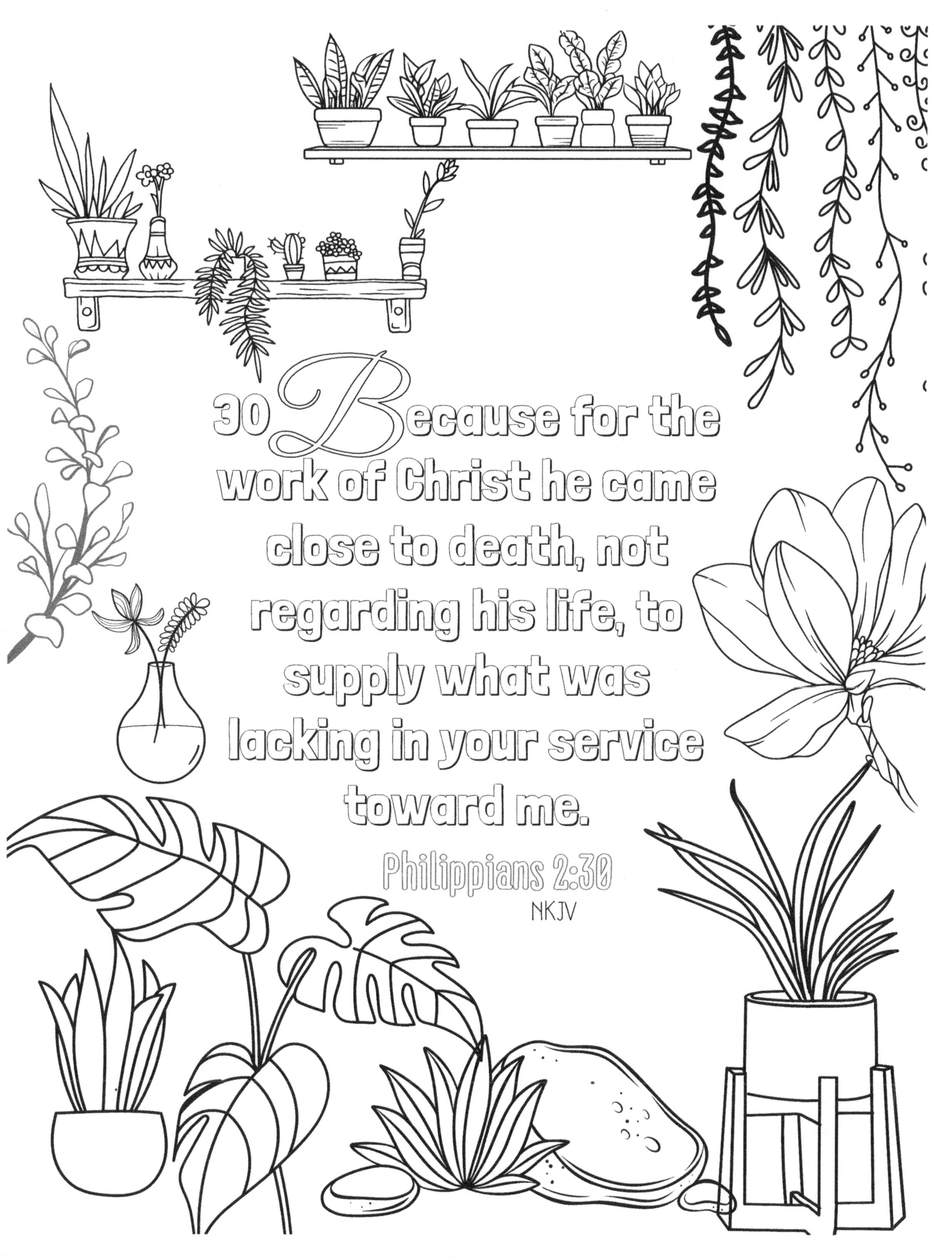
30 Because for the
work of Christ he came
close to death, not
regarding his life, to
supply what was
lacking in your service
toward me.
Philippians 2:30
NKJV

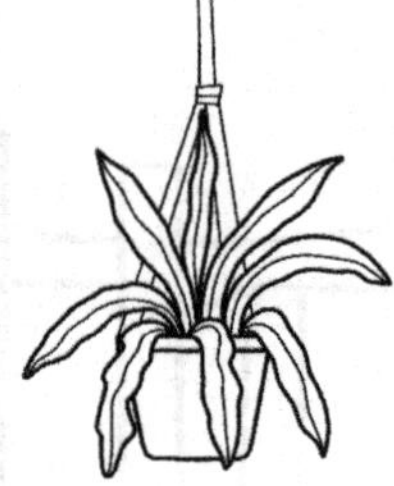

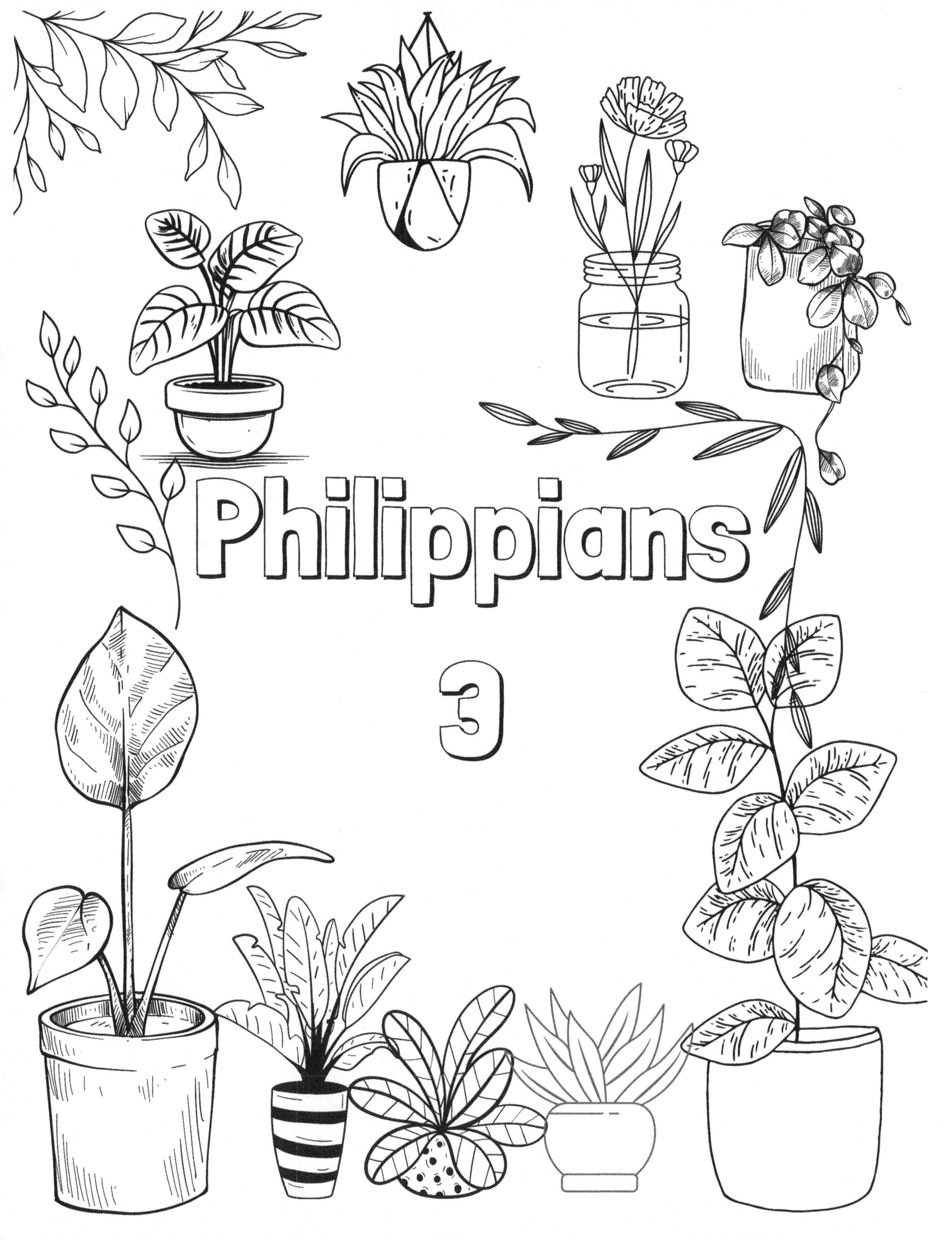
Philippians
3

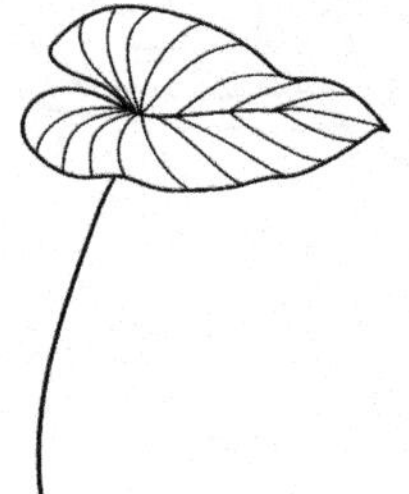

1. Finally, my brothers, rejoice in
the Lord! To write the same
things to you, to me indeed is not
tiresome, but for you it is safe. 2
Beware of the dogs; beware of
the evil workers; beware of the
false circumcision. 3 For we are
the circumcision, who worship
God in the Spirit, and rejoice in
Christ Jesus, and have no
confidence in the flesh;

Philippians 3:1–3 WEB

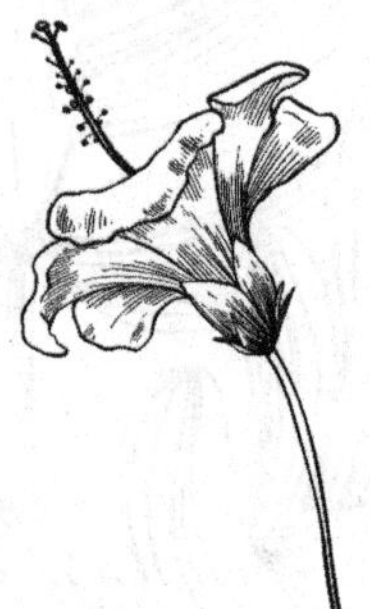

4 though I myself might have confidence
even in the flesh. If any other man thinks
that he has confidence in the flesh,
I yet more:
5 circumcised the eighth day, of the
stock of Israel, of the tribe of Benjamin,
a Hebrew of Hebrews; concerning the
law, a Pharisee;
6 concerning zeal, persecuting the
assembly; concerning the righteousness
which is in the law, found blameless.

Philippians 3:4–6

WEB

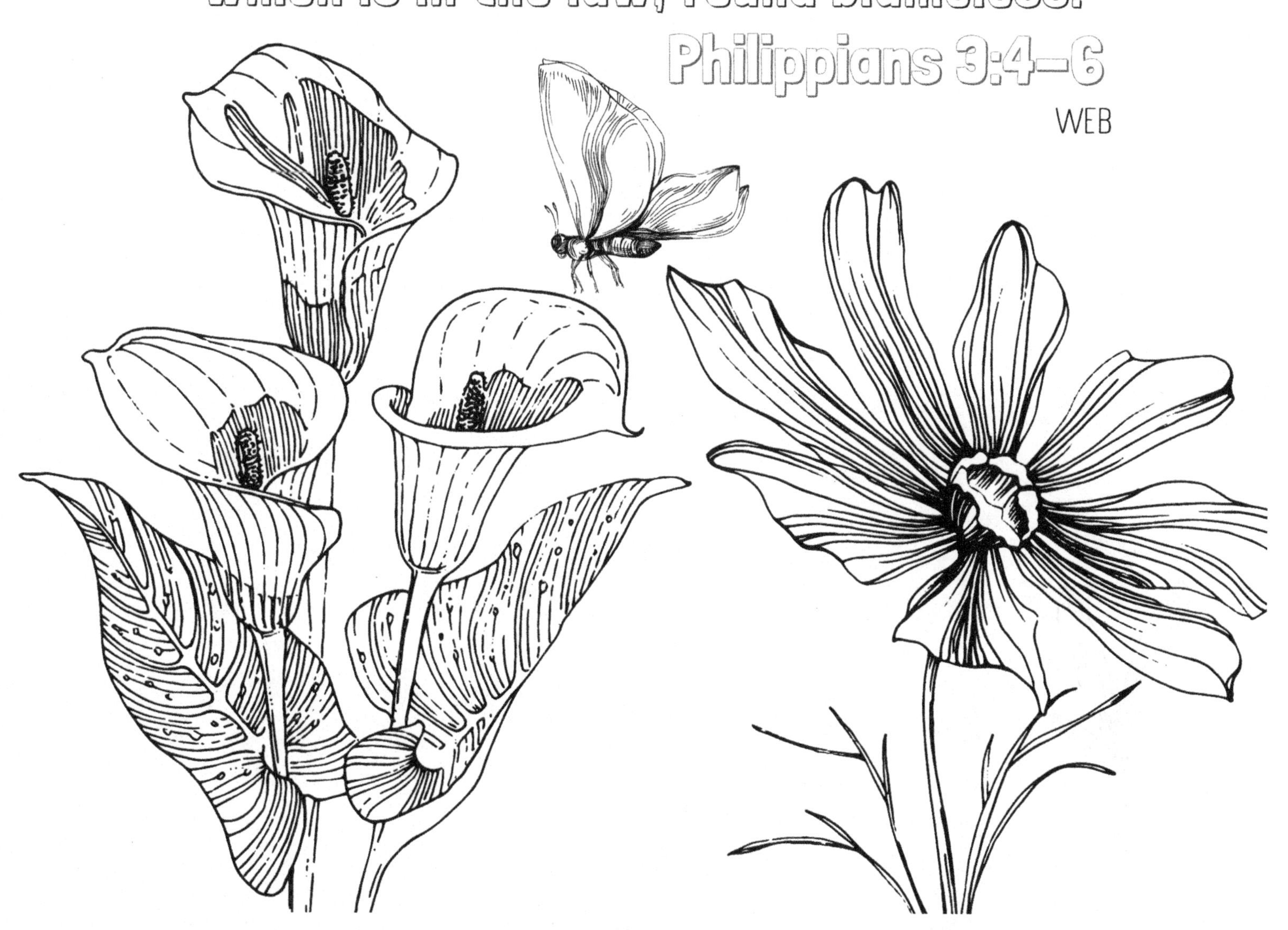

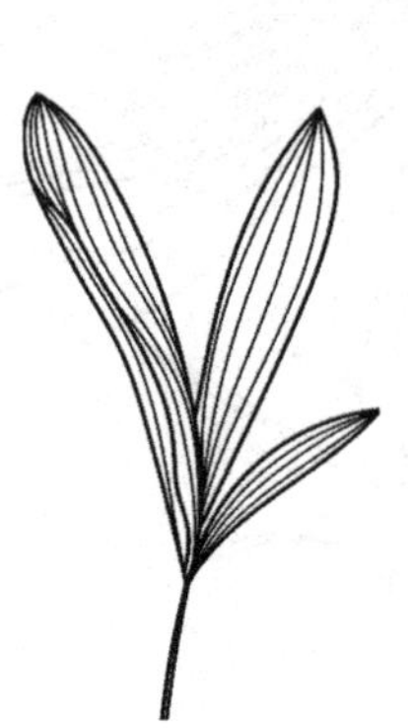

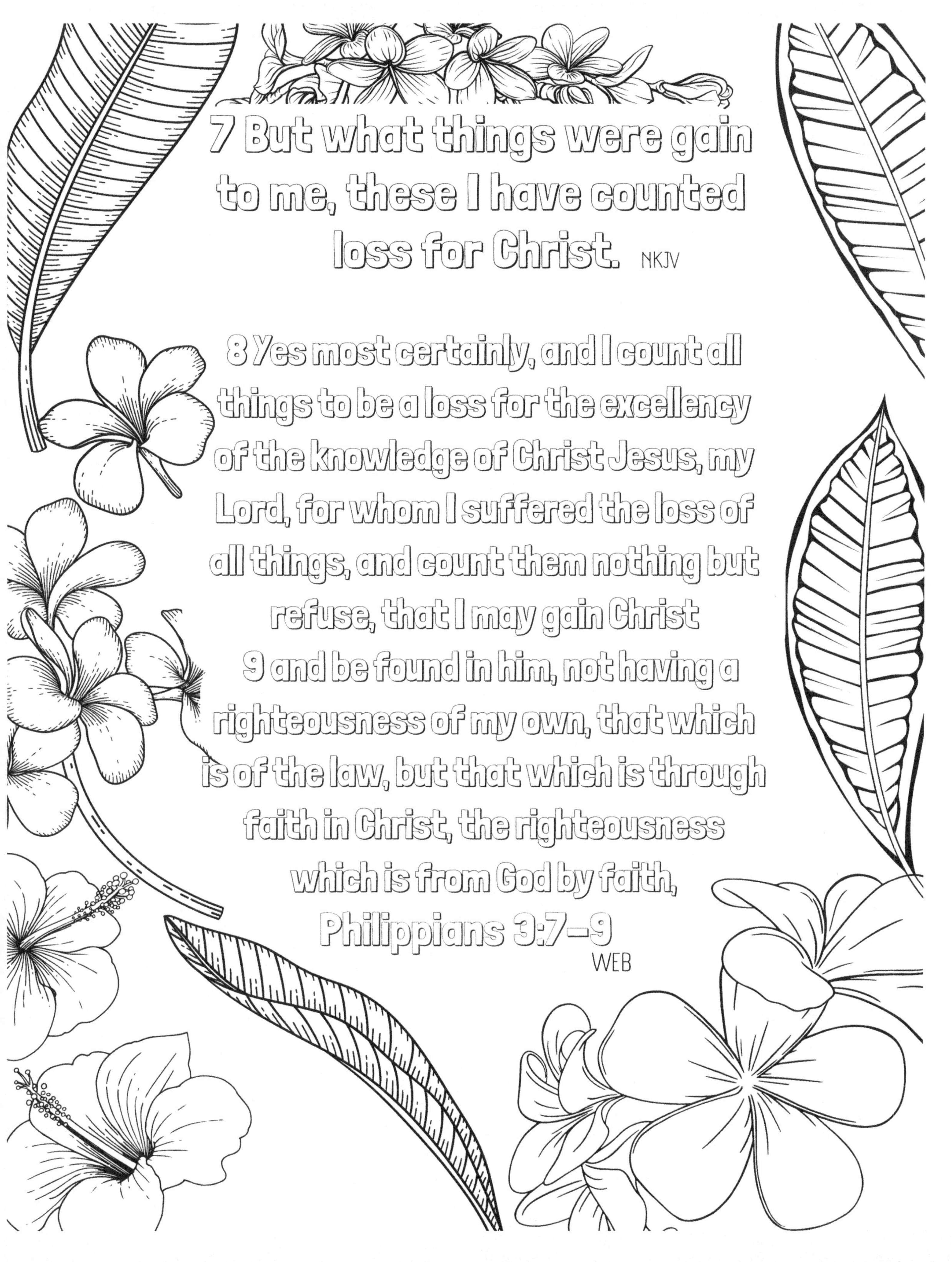
7 But what things were gain
to me, these I have counted
loss for Christ. NKJV
8 Yes most certainly, and I count all
things to be a loss for the excellency
of the knowledge of Christ Jesus, my
Lord, for whom I suffered the loss of
all things, and count them nothing but
refuse, that I may gain Christ
9 and be found in him, not having a
righteousness of my own, that which
is of the law, but that which is through
faith in Christ, the righteousness
which is from God by faith,
Philippians 3:7–9
WEB

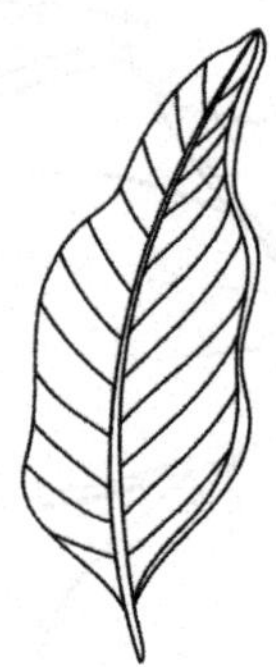

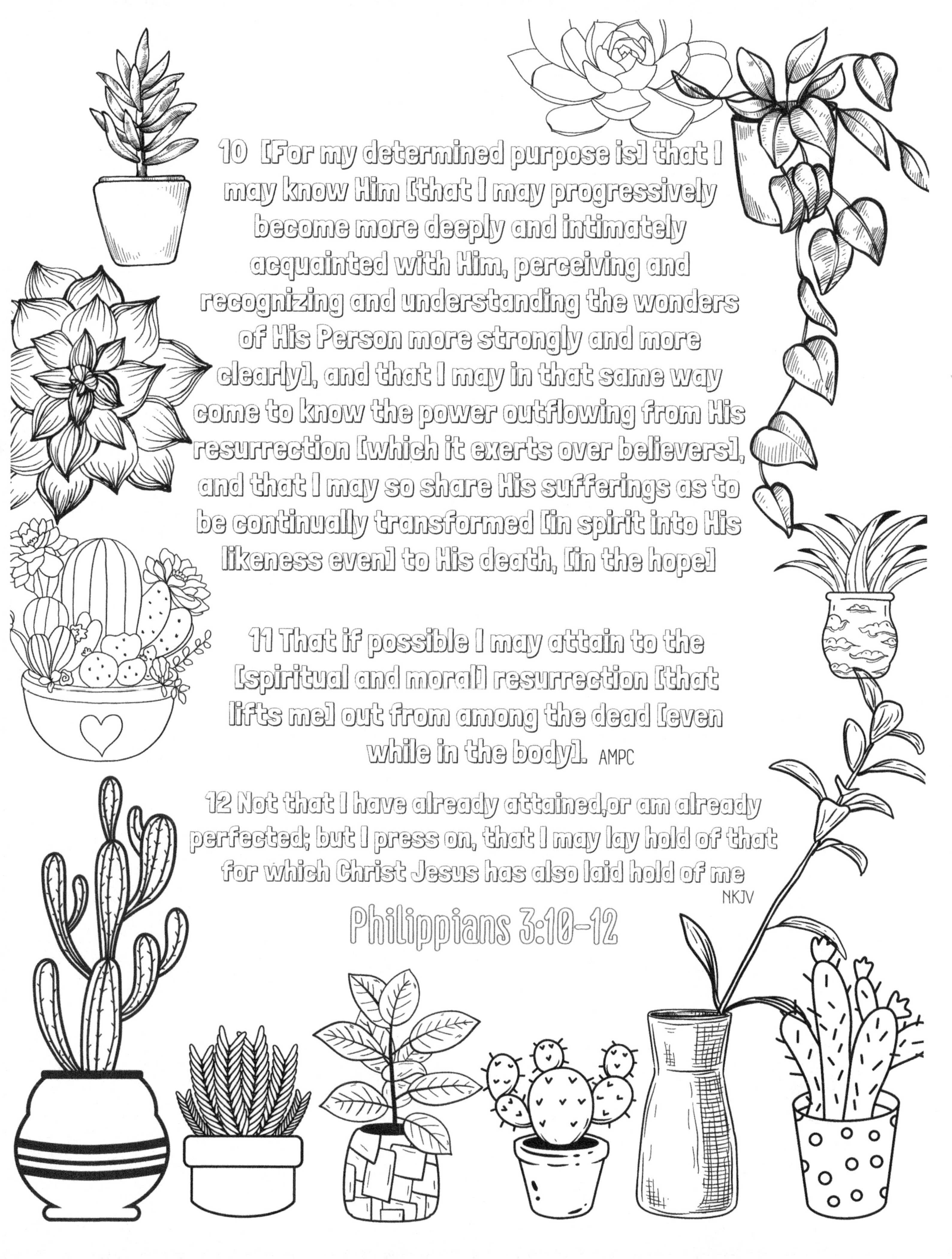
10 [For my determined purpose is] that I
may know Him [that I may progressively
become more deeply and intimately
acquainted with Him, perceiving and
recognizing and understanding the wonders
of His Person more strongly and more
clearly], and that I may in that same way
come to know the power outflowing from His
resurrection [which it exerts over believers],
and that I may so share His sufferings as to
be continually transformed [in spirit into His
likeness even] to His death, [in the hope]
11 That if possible I may attain to the
[spiritual and moral] resurrection [that
lifts me] out from among the dead [even
while in the body]. AMPC
12 Not that I have already attained,or am already
perfected; but I press on, that I may lay hold of that
for which Christ Jesus has also laid hold of me
NKJV
Philippians 3:10-12

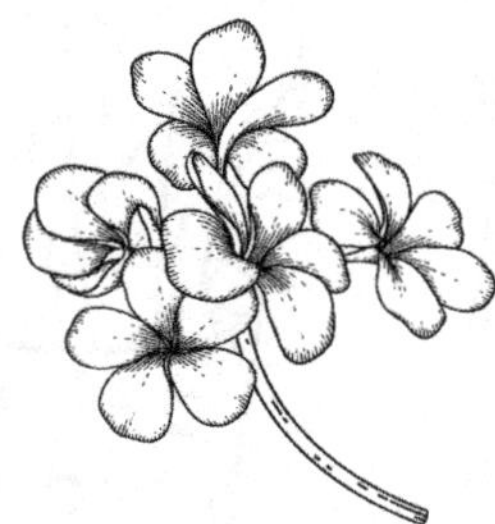

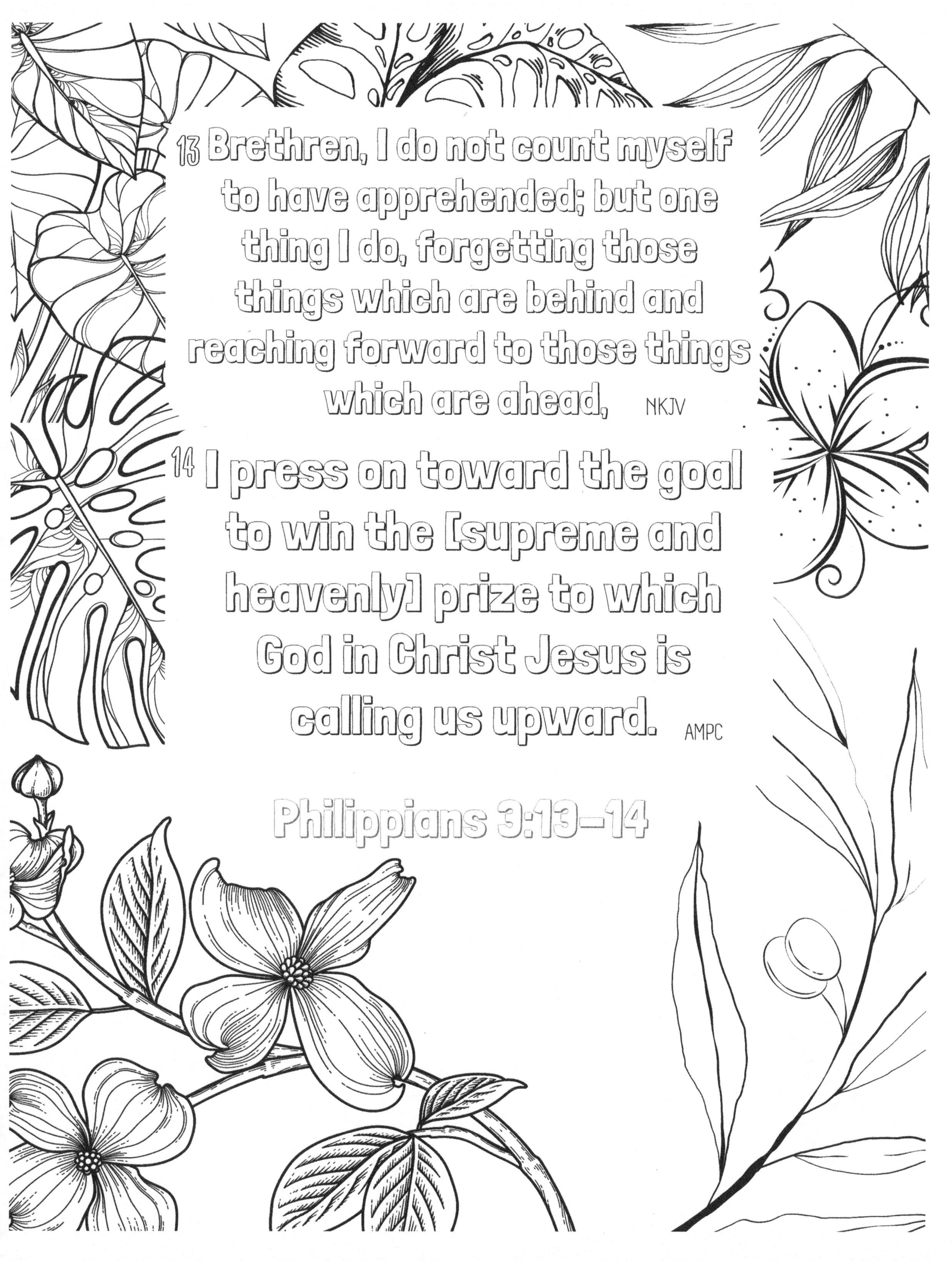
13 Brethren, I do not count myself
to have apprehended; but one
thing I do, forgetting those
things which are behind and
reaching forward to those things
which are ahead, NKJV
14 I press on toward the goal
to win the [supreme and
heavenly] prize to which
God in Christ Jesus is
calling us upward. AMPC
Philippians 3:13–14

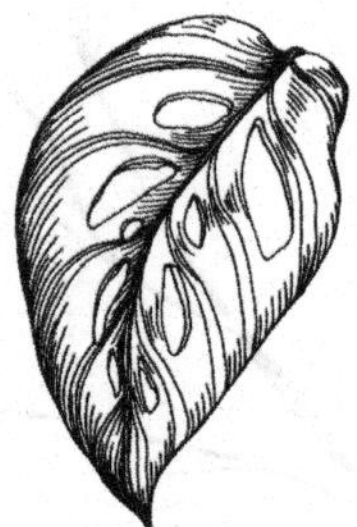

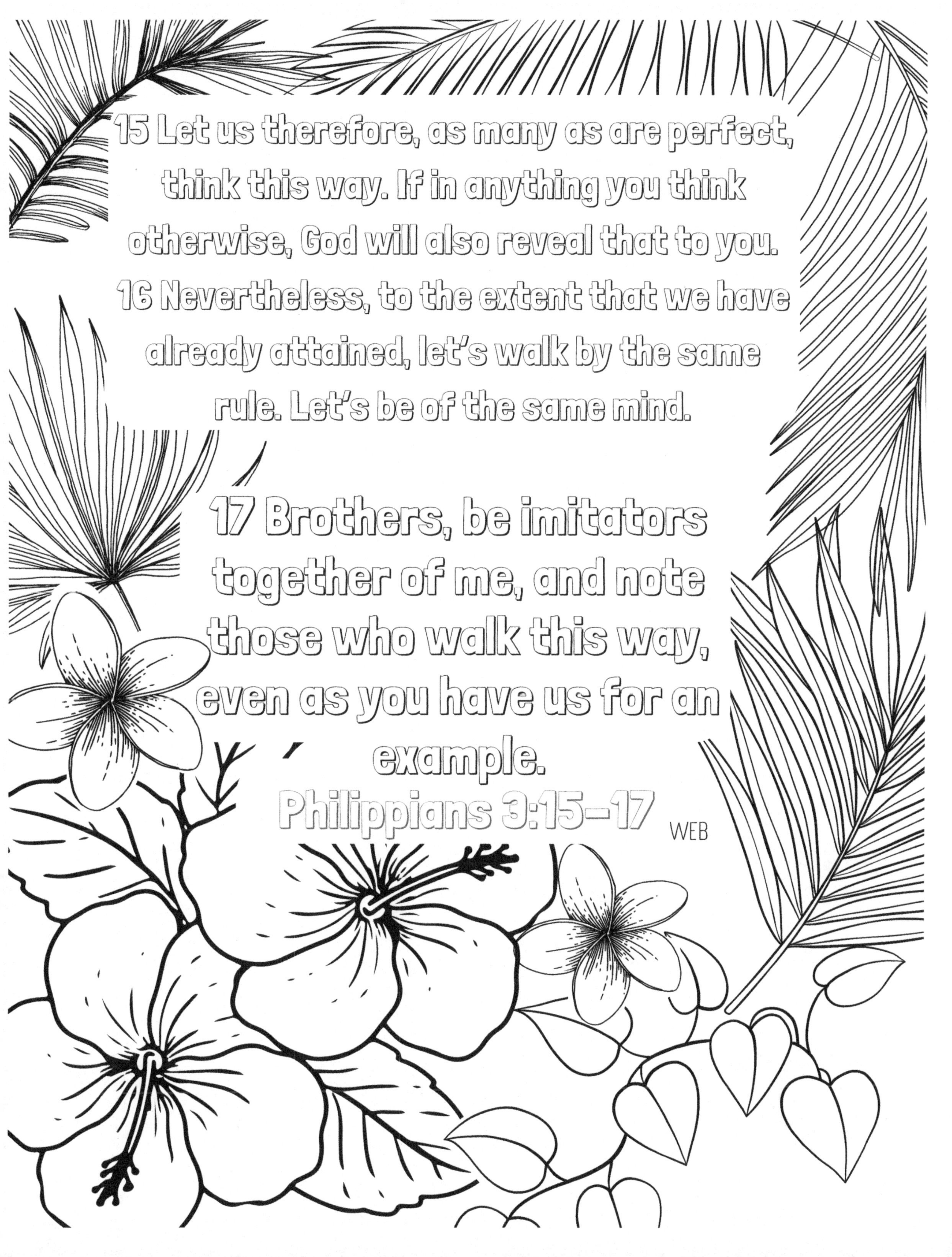
15 Let us therefore, as many as are perfect,
think this way. If in anything you think
otherwise, God will also reveal that to you.
16 Nevertheless, to the extent that we have
already attained, let's walk by the same
rule. Let's be of the same mind.
17 Brothers, be imitators
together of me, and note
those who walk this way,
even as you have us for an
example.
Philippians 3:15–17
WEB

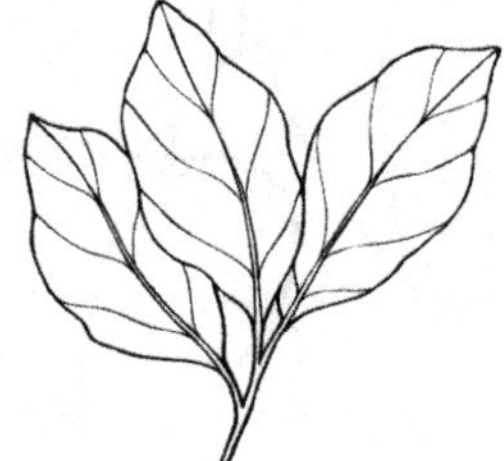

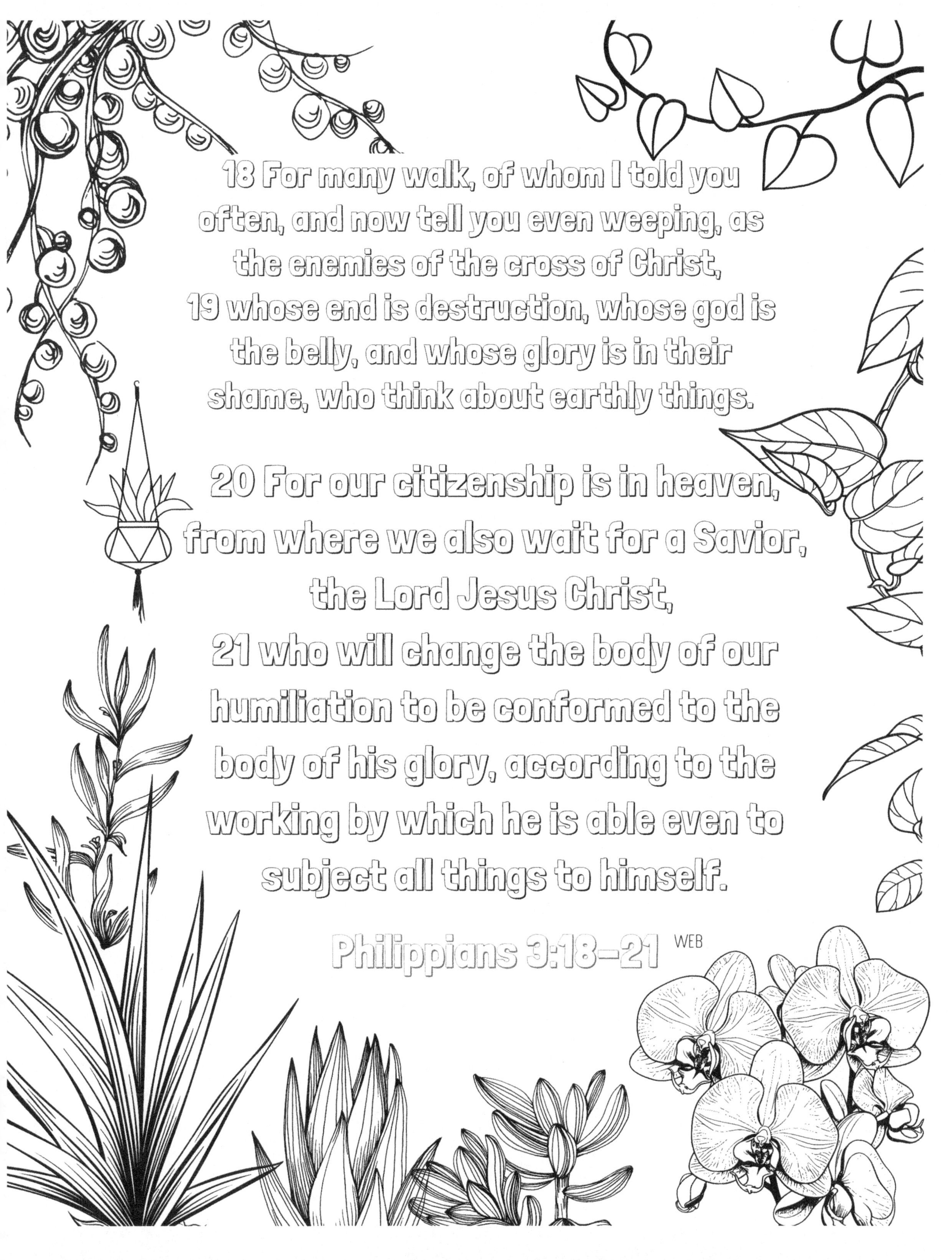
18 For many walk, of whom I told you
often, and now tell you even weeping, as
the enemies of the cross of Christ,
19 whose end is destruction, whose god is
the belly, and whose glory is in their
shame, who think about earthly things.
20 For our citizenship is in heaven,
from where we also wait for a Savior,
the Lord Jesus Christ,
21 who will change the body of our
humiliation to be conformed to the
body of his glory, according to the
working by which he is able even to
subject all things to himself.
Philippians 3:18–21 WEB

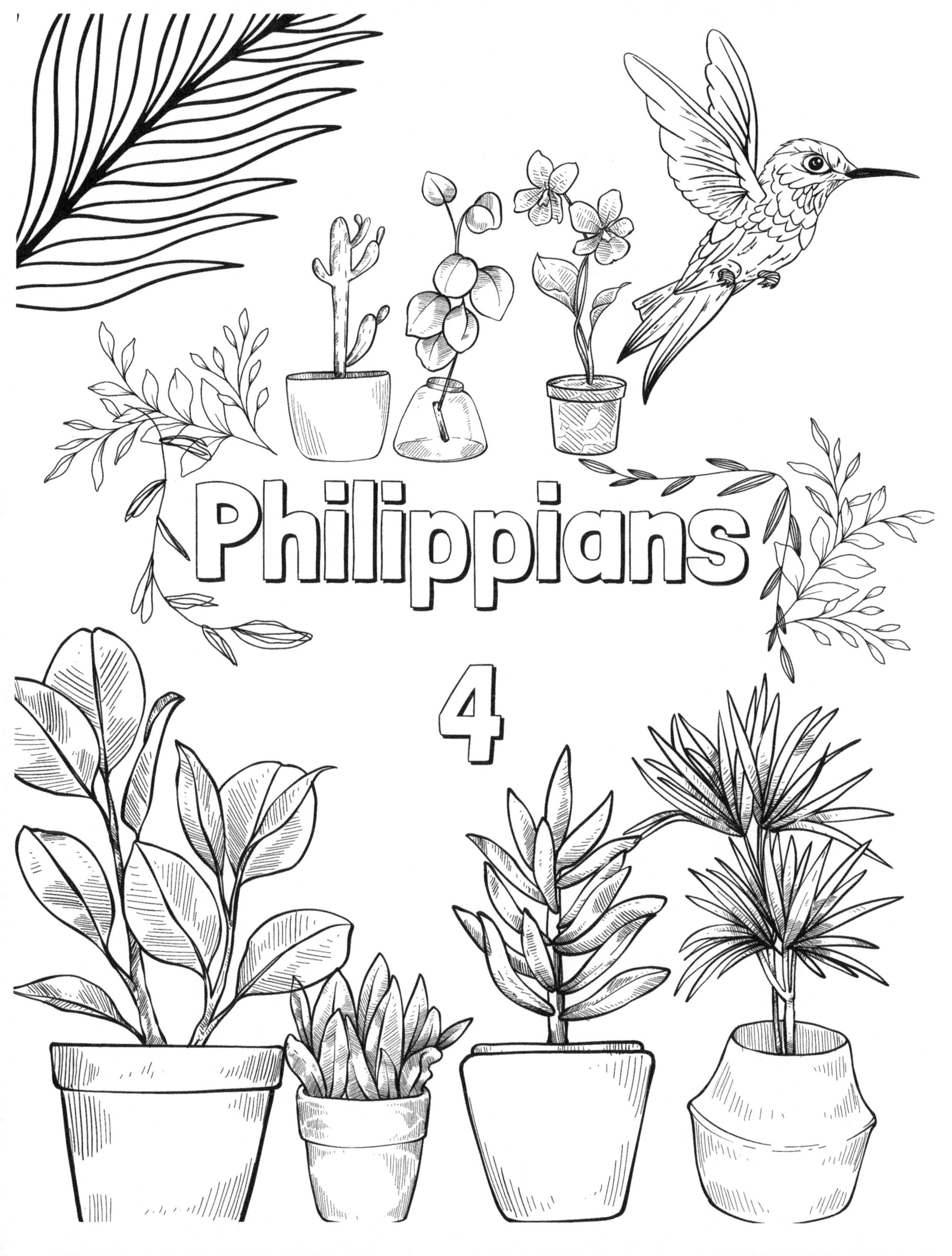
Philippians
4

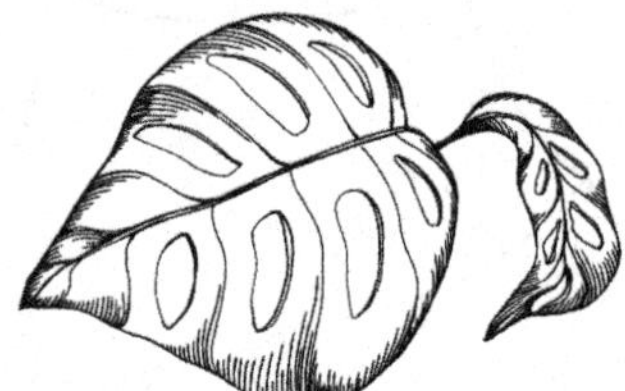

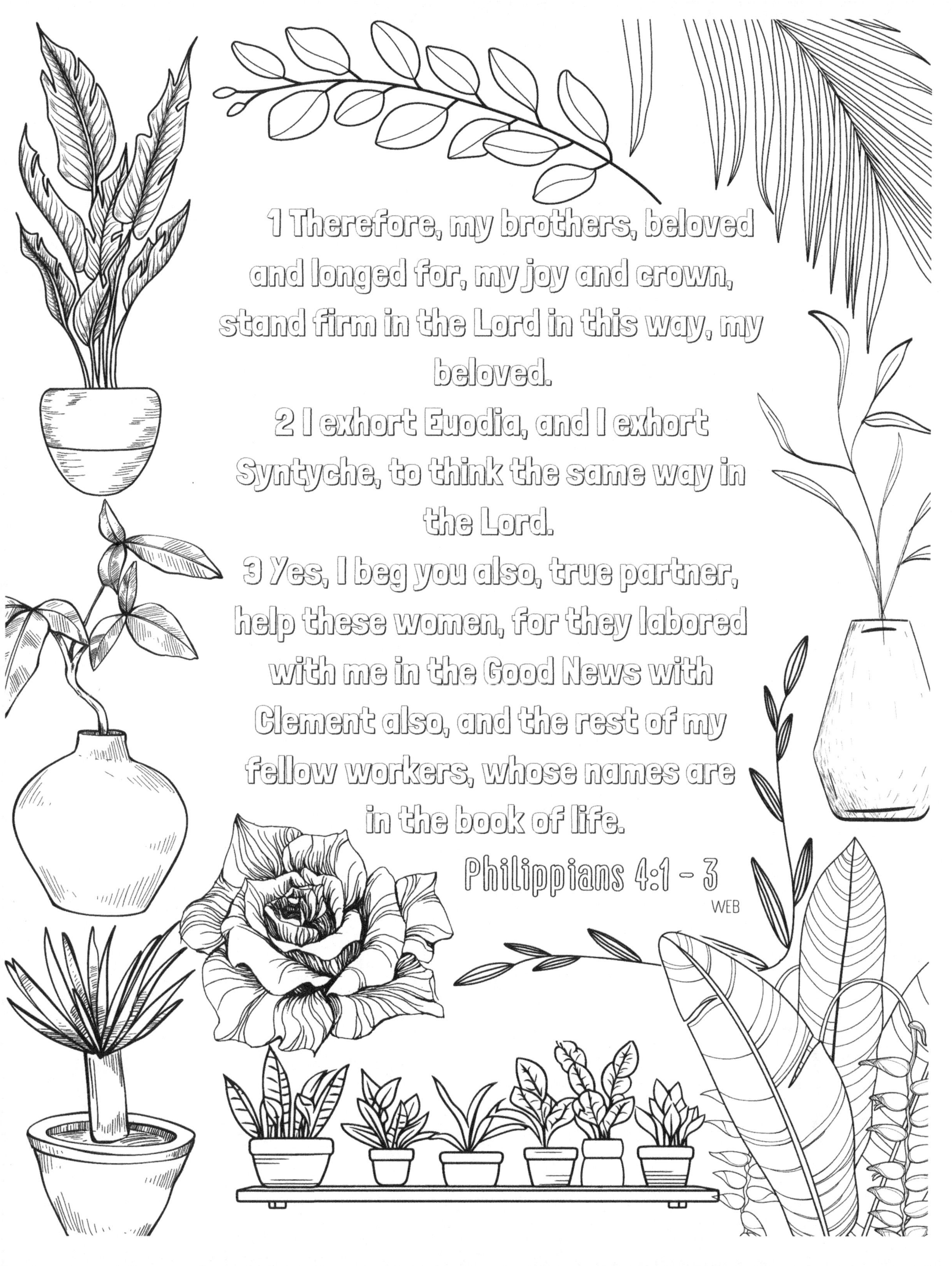
1 Therefore, my brothers, beloved
and longed for, my joy and crown,
stand firm in the Lord in this way, my
beloved.
2 I exhort Euodia, and I exhort
Syntyche, to think the same way in
the Lord.
3 Yes, I beg you also, true partner,
help these women, for they labored
with me in the Good News with
Clement also, and the rest of my
fellow workers, whose names are
in the book of life.
Philippians 4:1 - 3
WEB

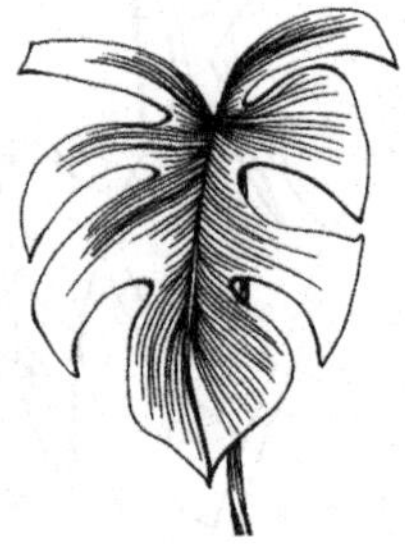

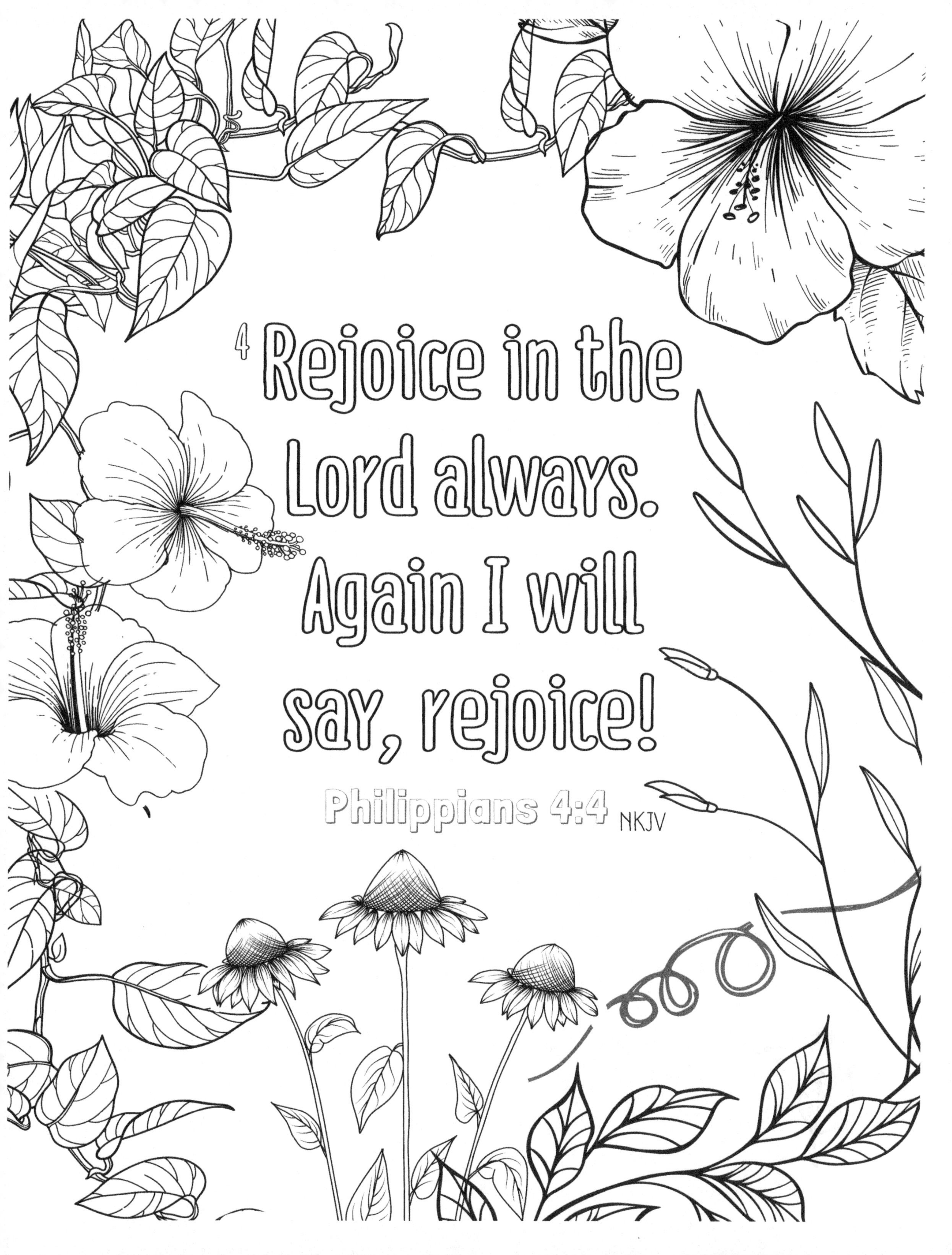
4 Rejoice in the
Lord always.
Again I will
say, rejoice!
Philippians 4:4 NKJV

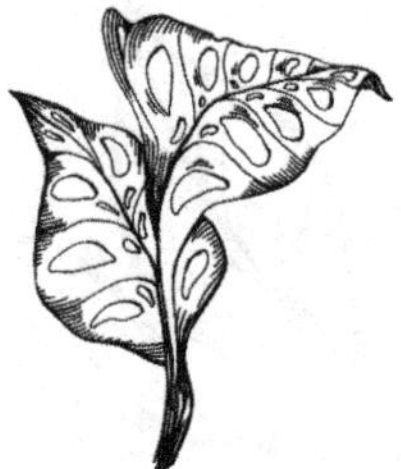

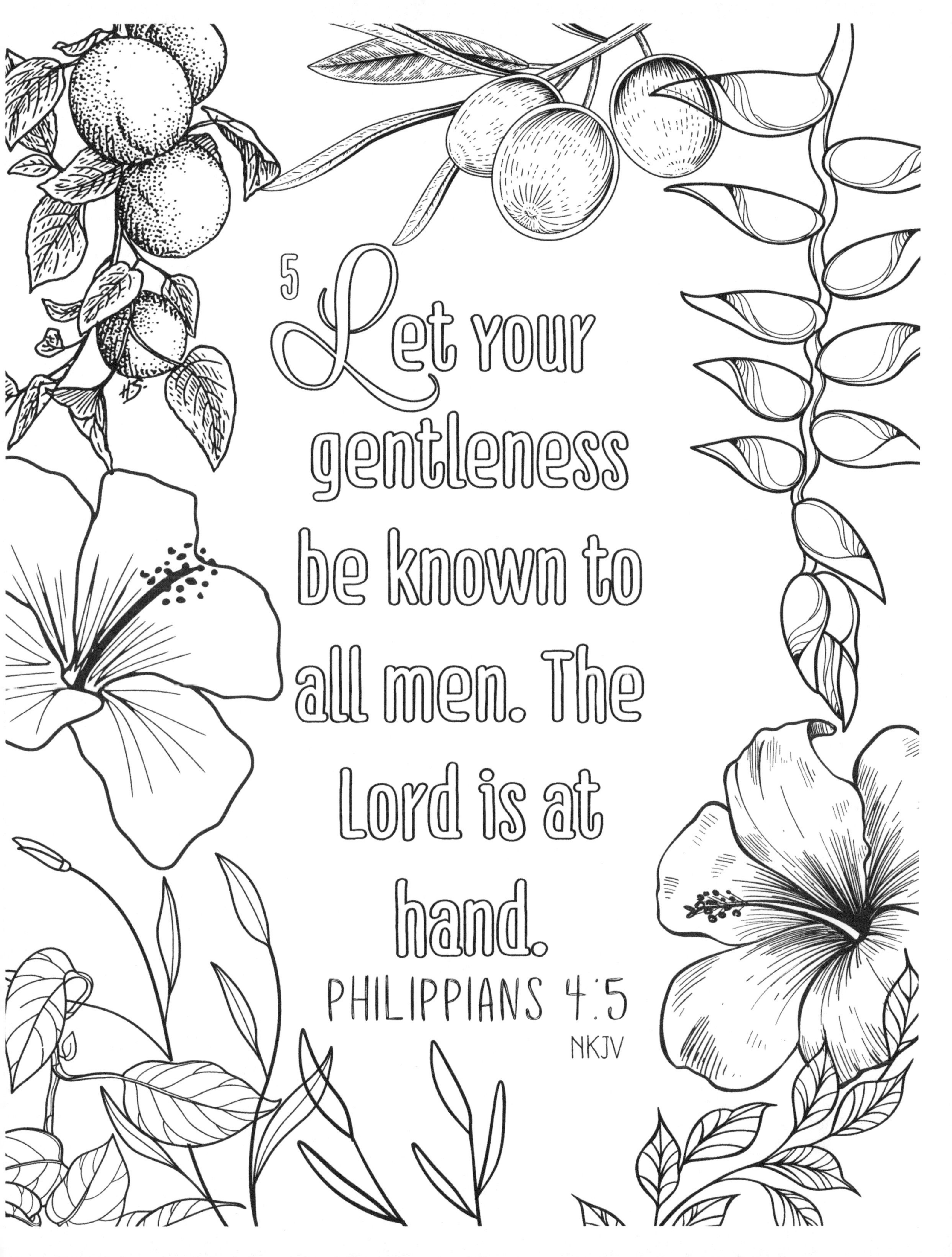
5 Let your gentleness be known to all men. The Lord is at hand.
PHILIPPIANS 4:5
NKJV

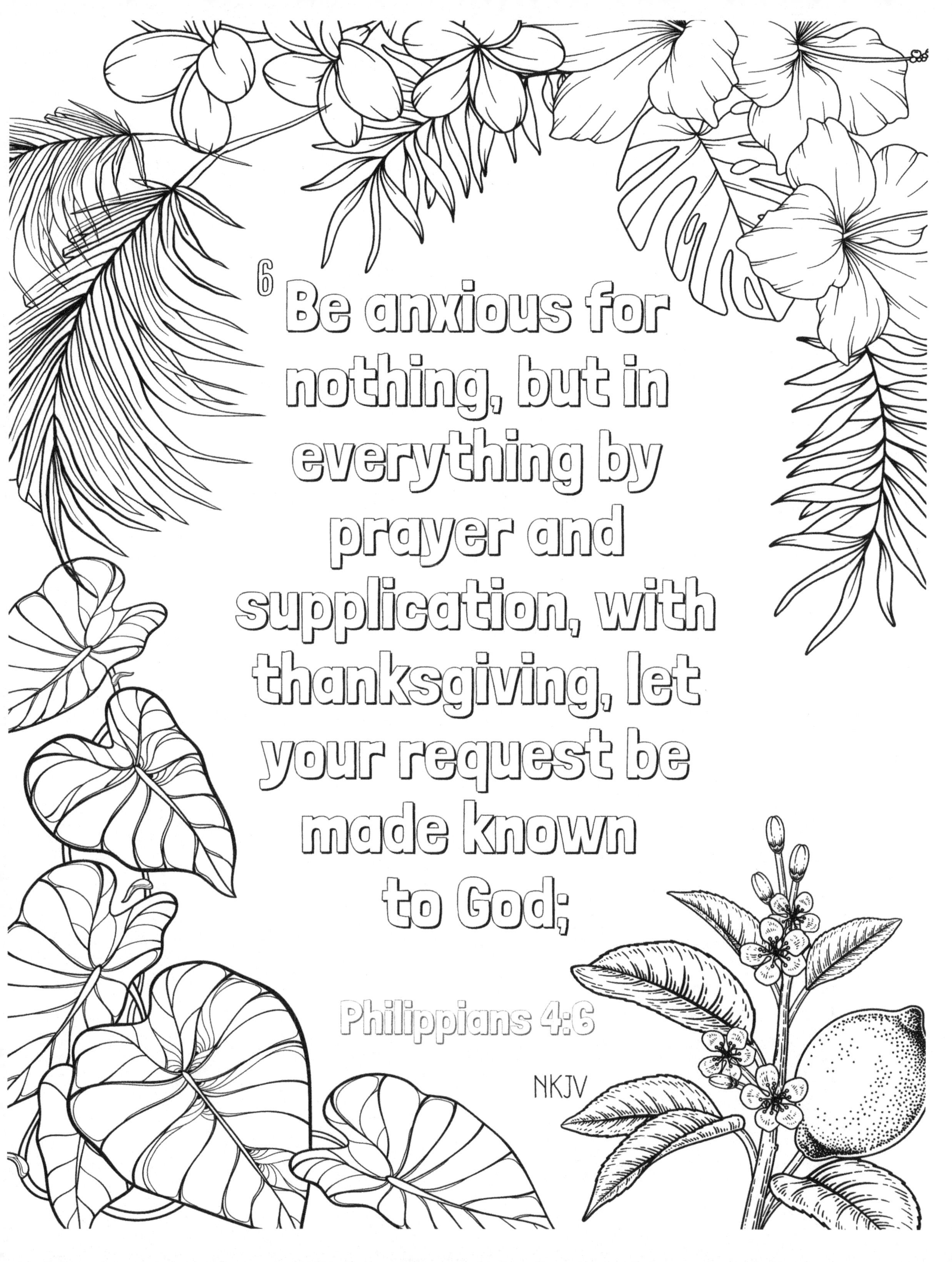

6 Be anxious for
nothing, but in
everything by
prayer and
supplication, with
thanksgiving, let
your request be
made known
to God;
Philippians 4:6
NKJV

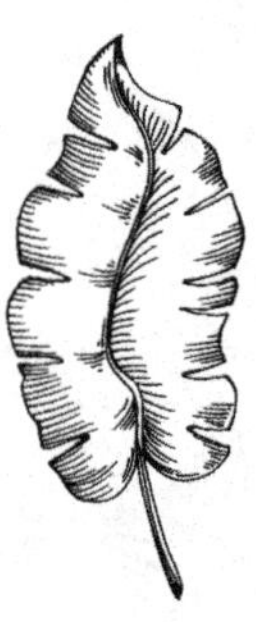

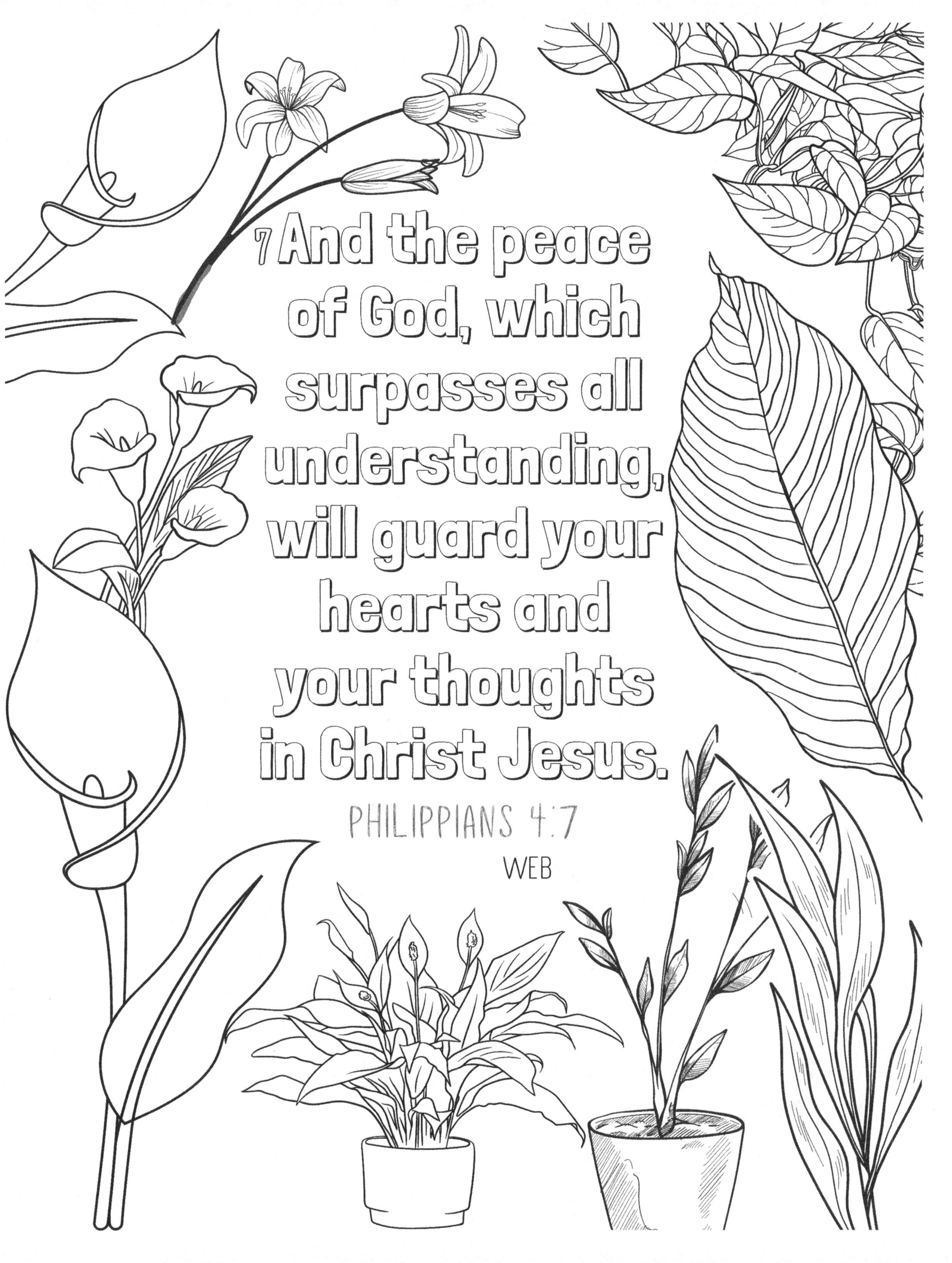
7 And the peace
of God, which
surpasses all
understanding,
will guard your
hearts and
your thoughts
in Christ Jesus.
PHILIPPIANS 4:7
WEB

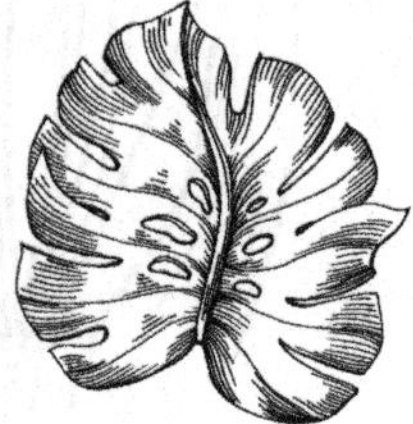

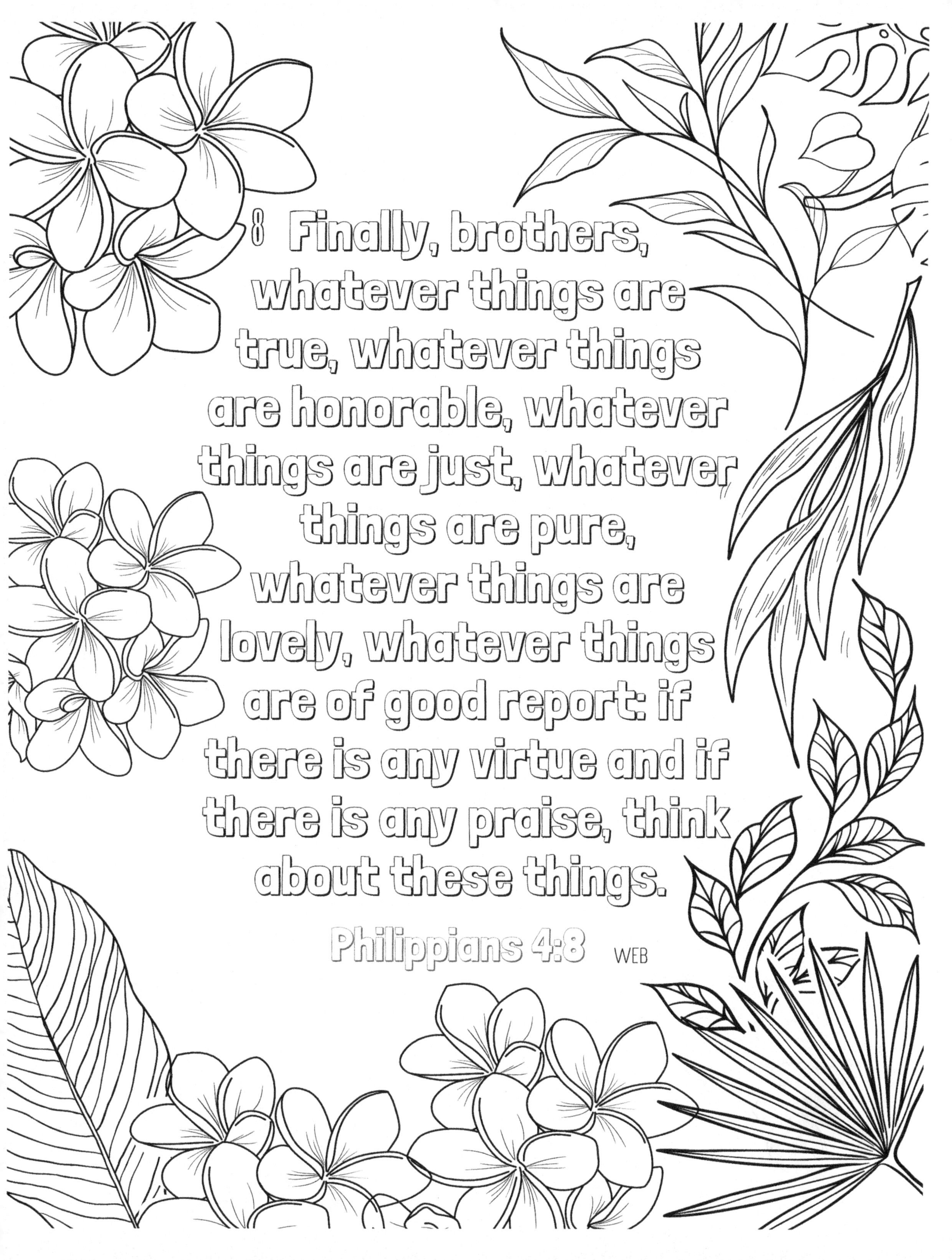
8 Finally, brothers,
whatever things are
true, whatever things
are honorable, whatever
things are just, whatever
things are pure,
whatever things are
lovely, whatever things
are of good report: if
there is any virtue and if
there is any praise, think
about these things.
Philippians 4:8 WEB

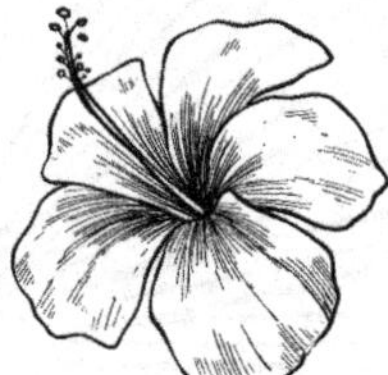

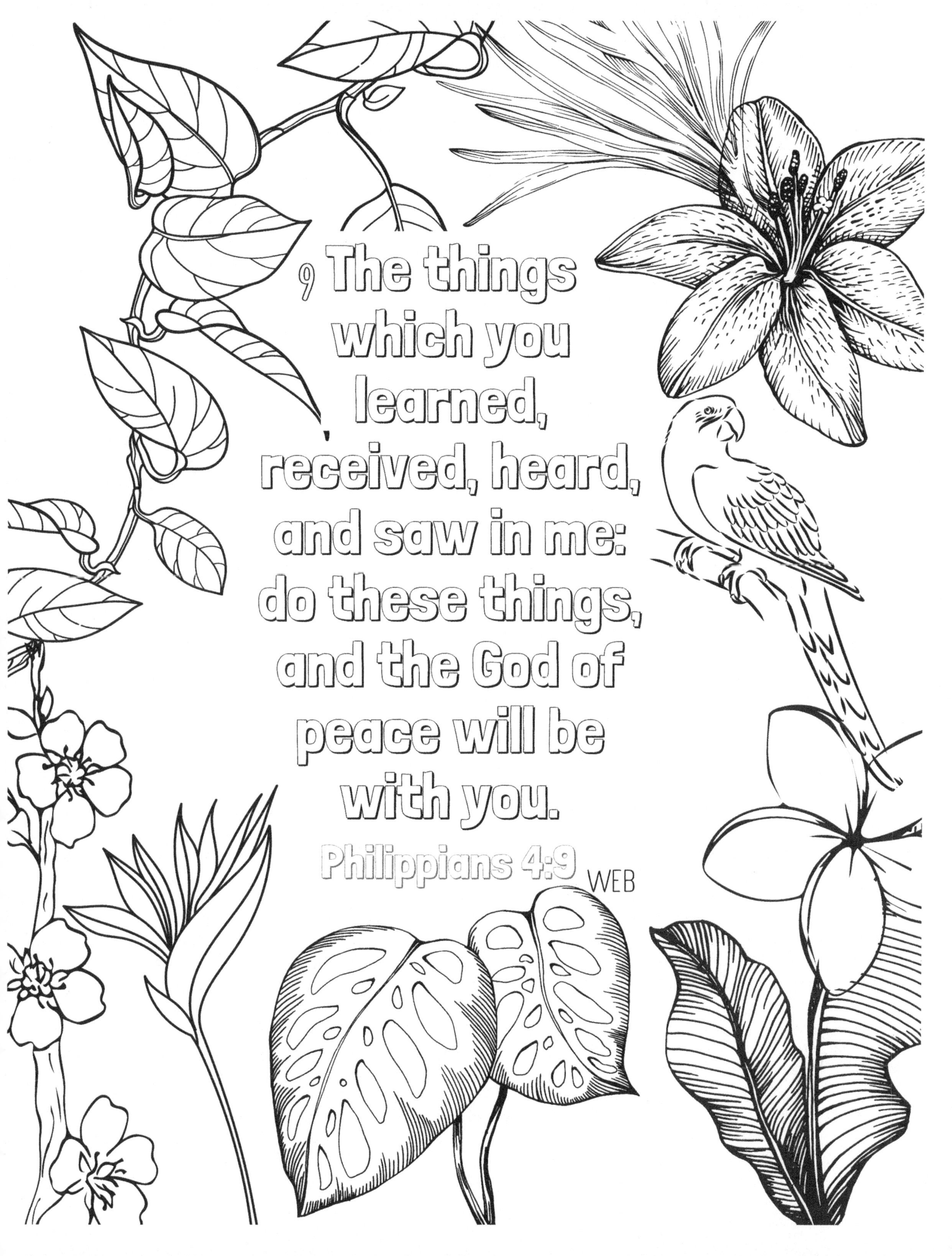
9 The things
which you
learned,
received, heard,
and saw in me:
do these things,
and the God of
peace will be
with you.
Philippians 4:9 WEB

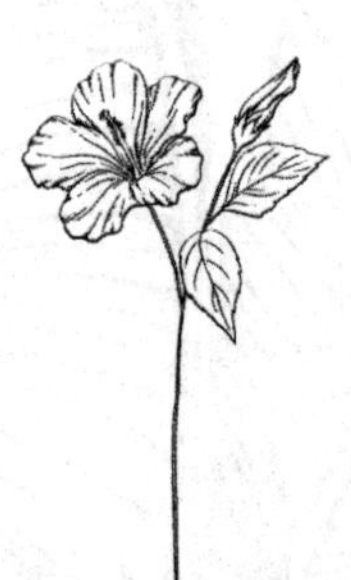

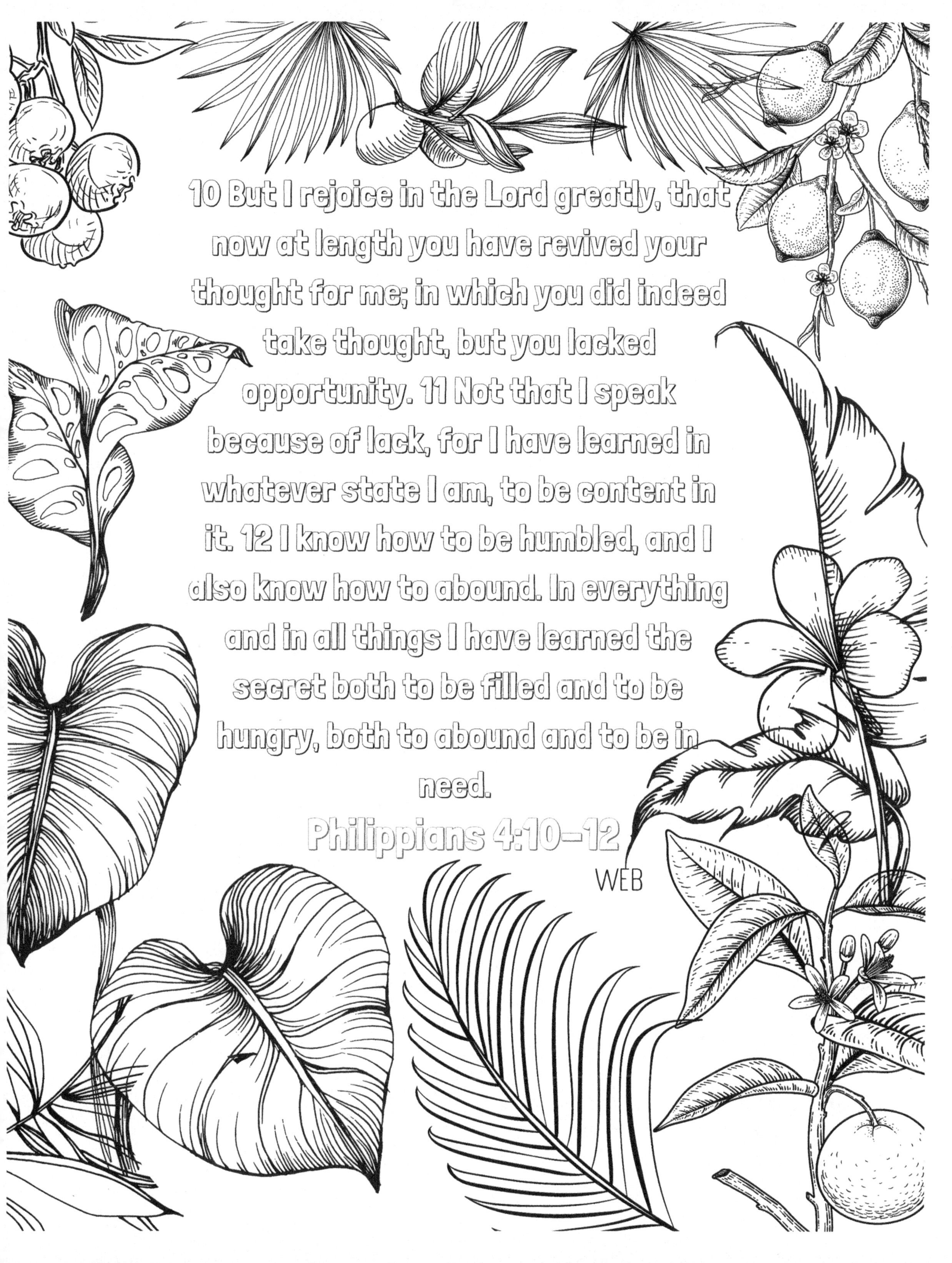
10 But I rejoice in the Lord greatly, that
now at length you have revived your
thought for me; in which you did indeed
take thought, but you lacked
opportunity. 11 Not that I speak
because of lack, for I have learned in
whatever state I am, to be content in
it. 12 I know how to be humbled, and I
also know how to abound. In everything
and in all things I have learned the
secret both to be filled and to be
hungry, both to abound and to be in
need.
Philippians 4:10–12
WEB

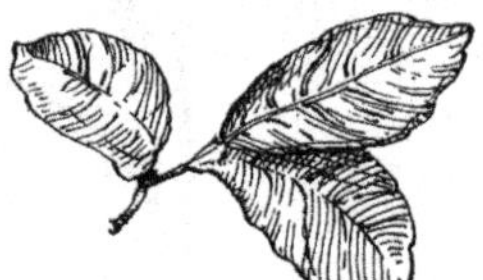

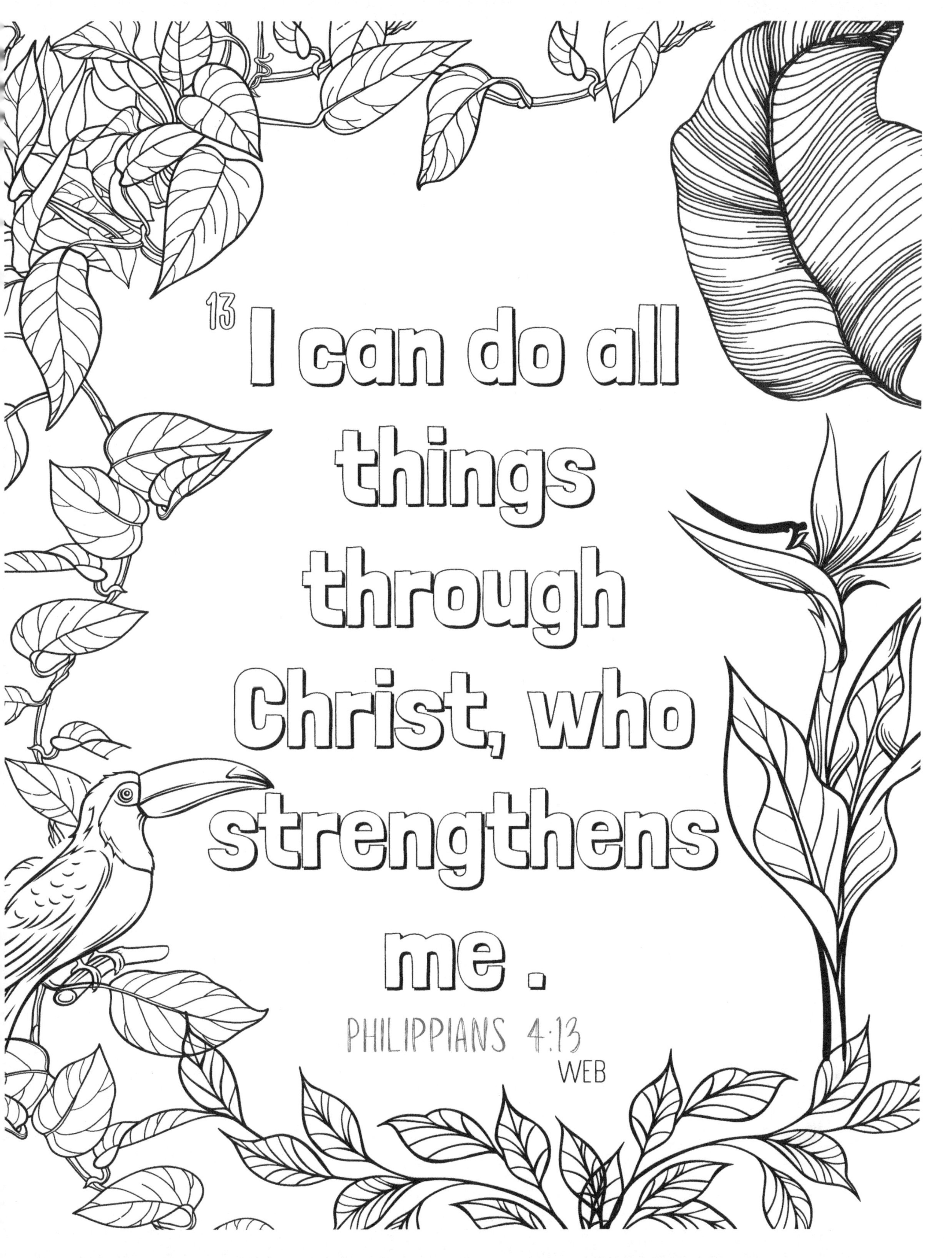
13 I can do all things through Christ, who strengthens me .
PHILIPPIANS 4:13
WEB

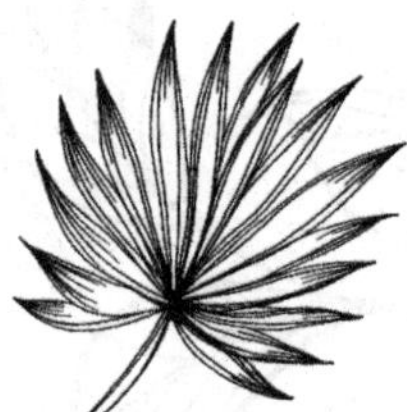

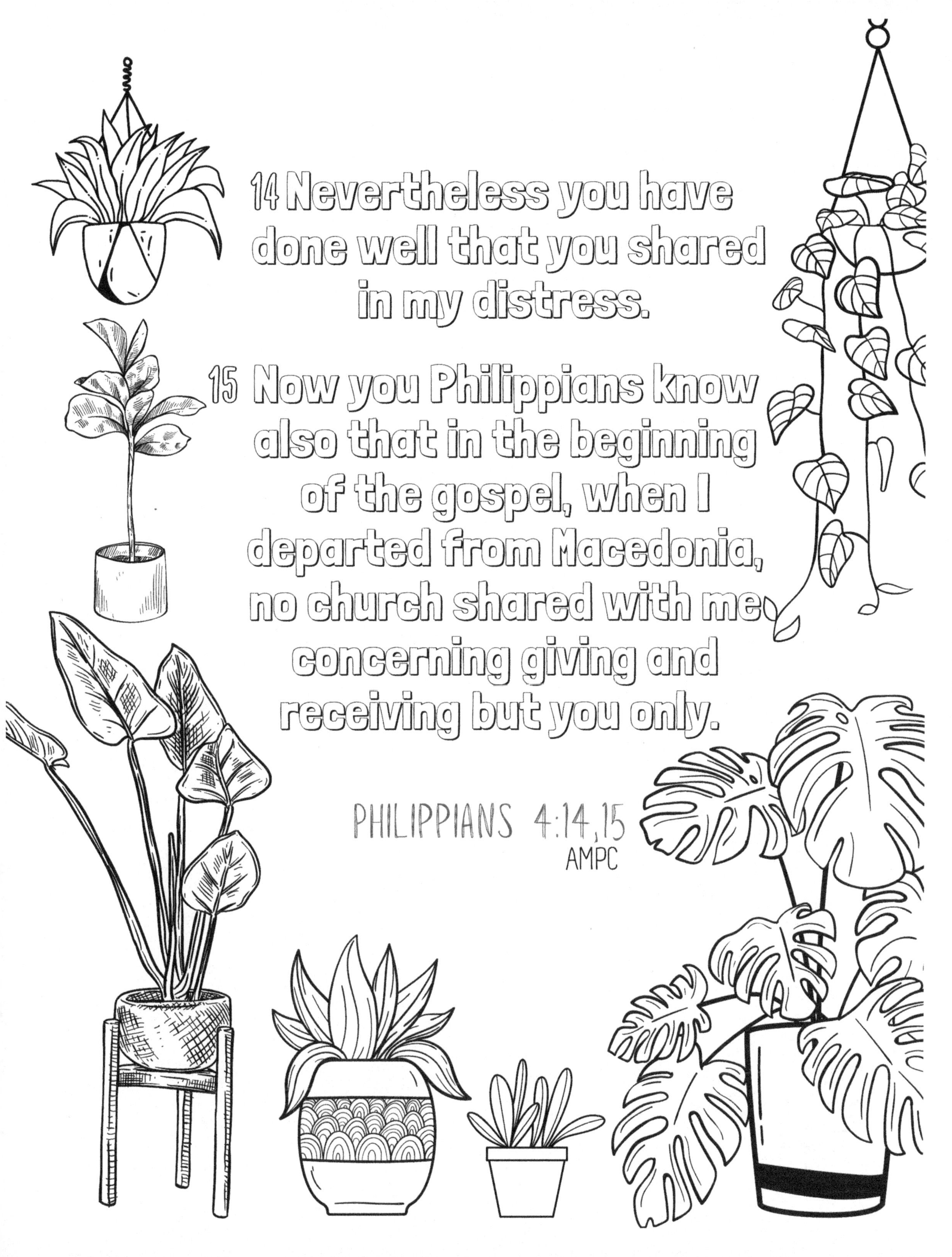
14 Nevertheless you have
done well that you shared
in my distress.
15 Now you Philippians know
also that in the beginning
of the gospel, when I
departed from Macedonia,
no church shared with me
concerning giving and
receiving but you only.
PHILIPPIANS 4:14,15
AMPC

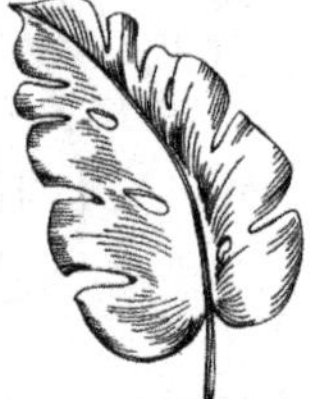

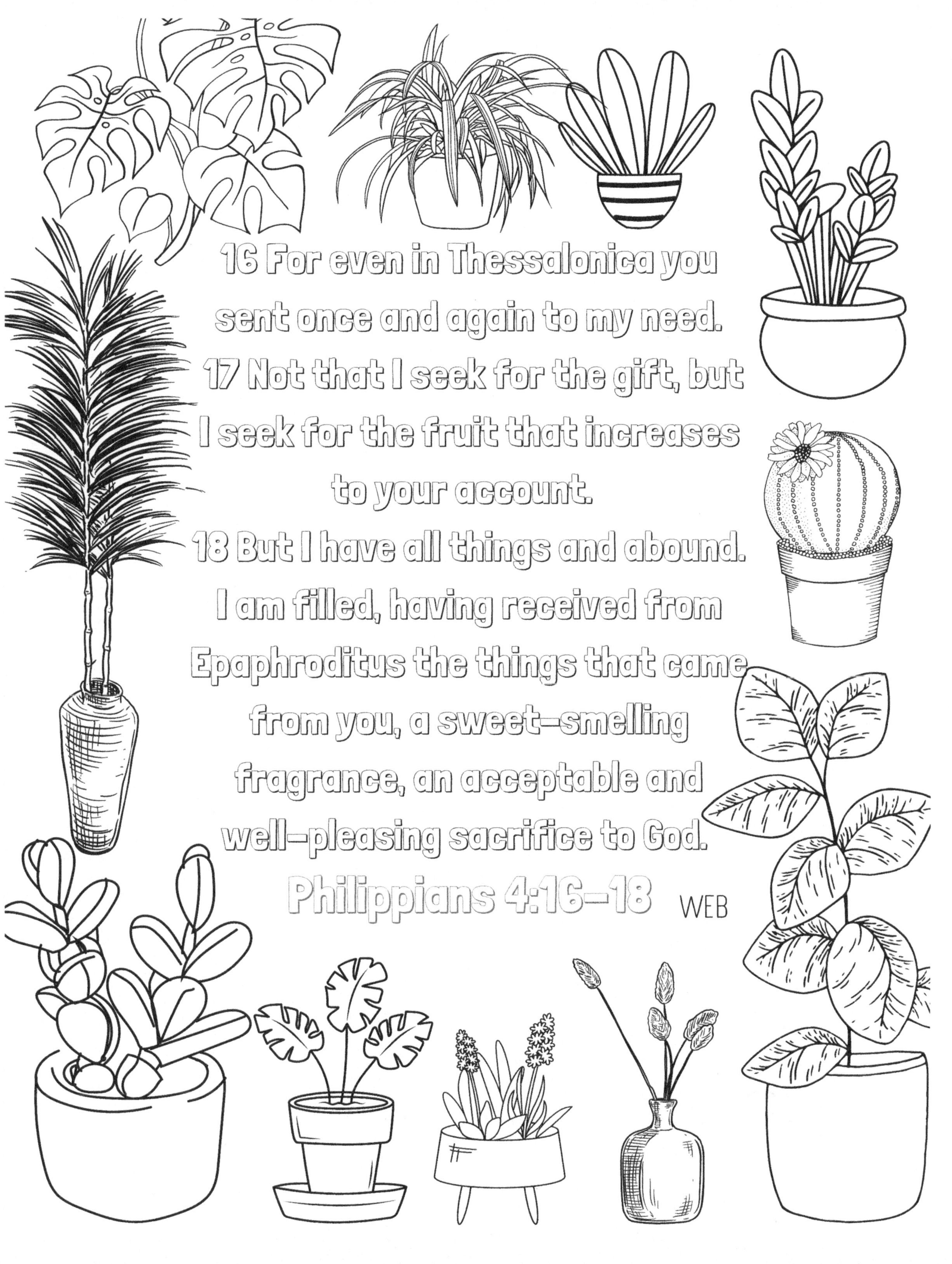
16 For even in Thessalonica you
sent once and again to my need.
17 Not that I seek for the gift, but
I seek for the fruit that increases
to your account.
18 But I have all things and abound.
I am filled, having received from
Epaphroditus the things that came
from you, a sweet-smelling
fragrance, an acceptable and
well-pleasing sacrifice to God.
Philippians 4:16-18
WEB

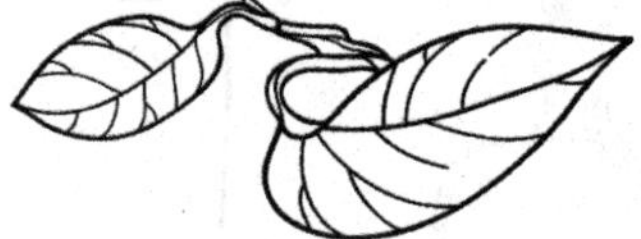

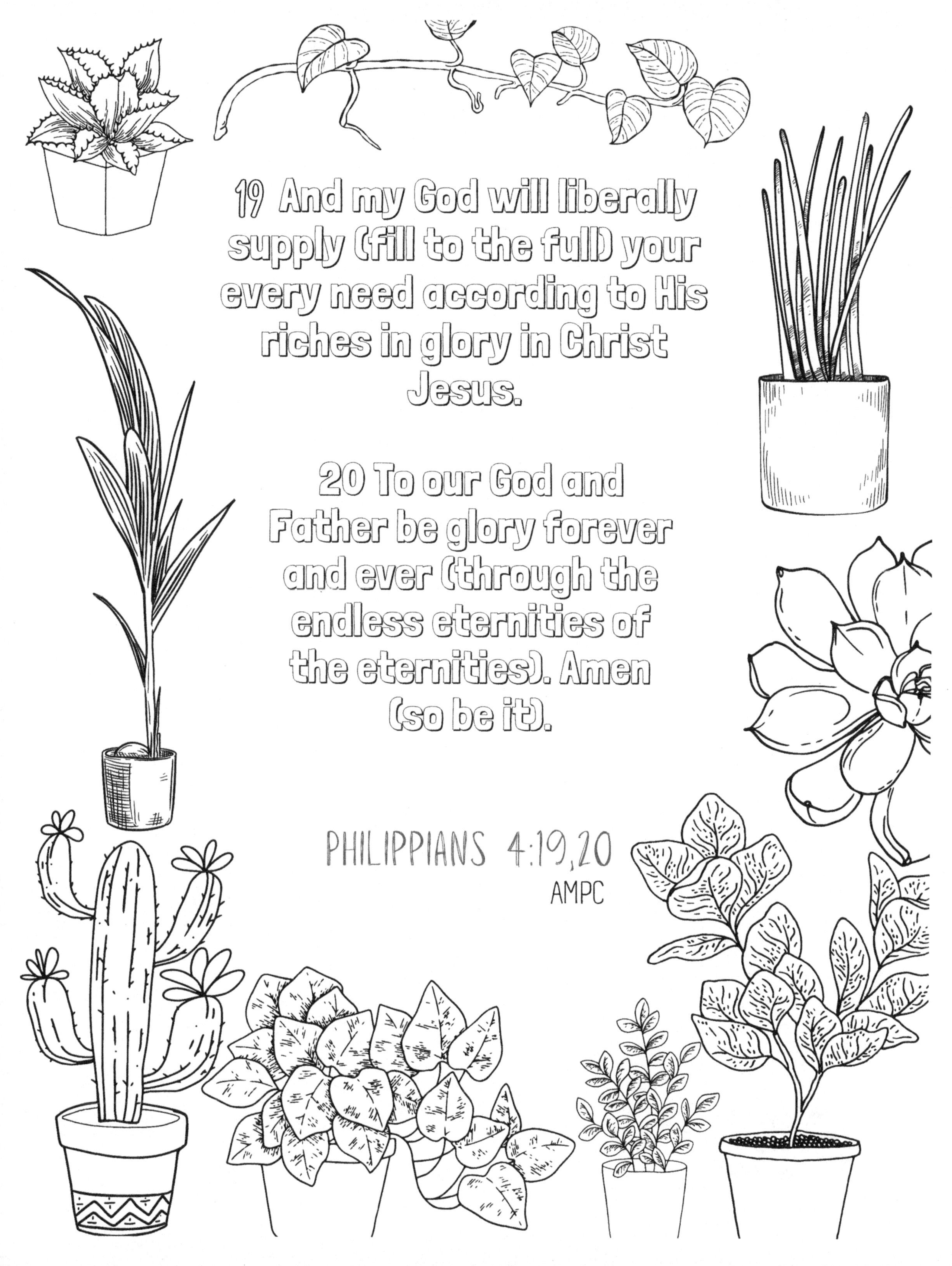
19 And my God will liberally
supply (fill to the full) your
every need according to His
riches in glory in Christ
Jesus.
20 To our God and
Father be glory forever
and ever (through the
endless eternities of
the eternities). Amen
(so be it).
PHILIPPIANS 4:19,20
AMPC

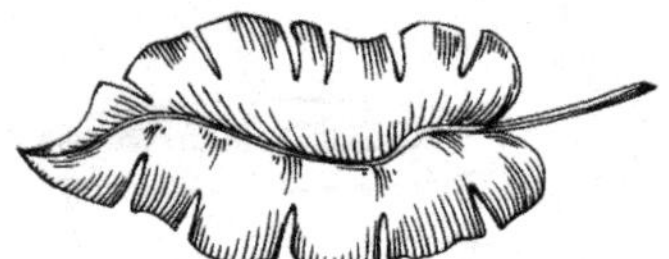

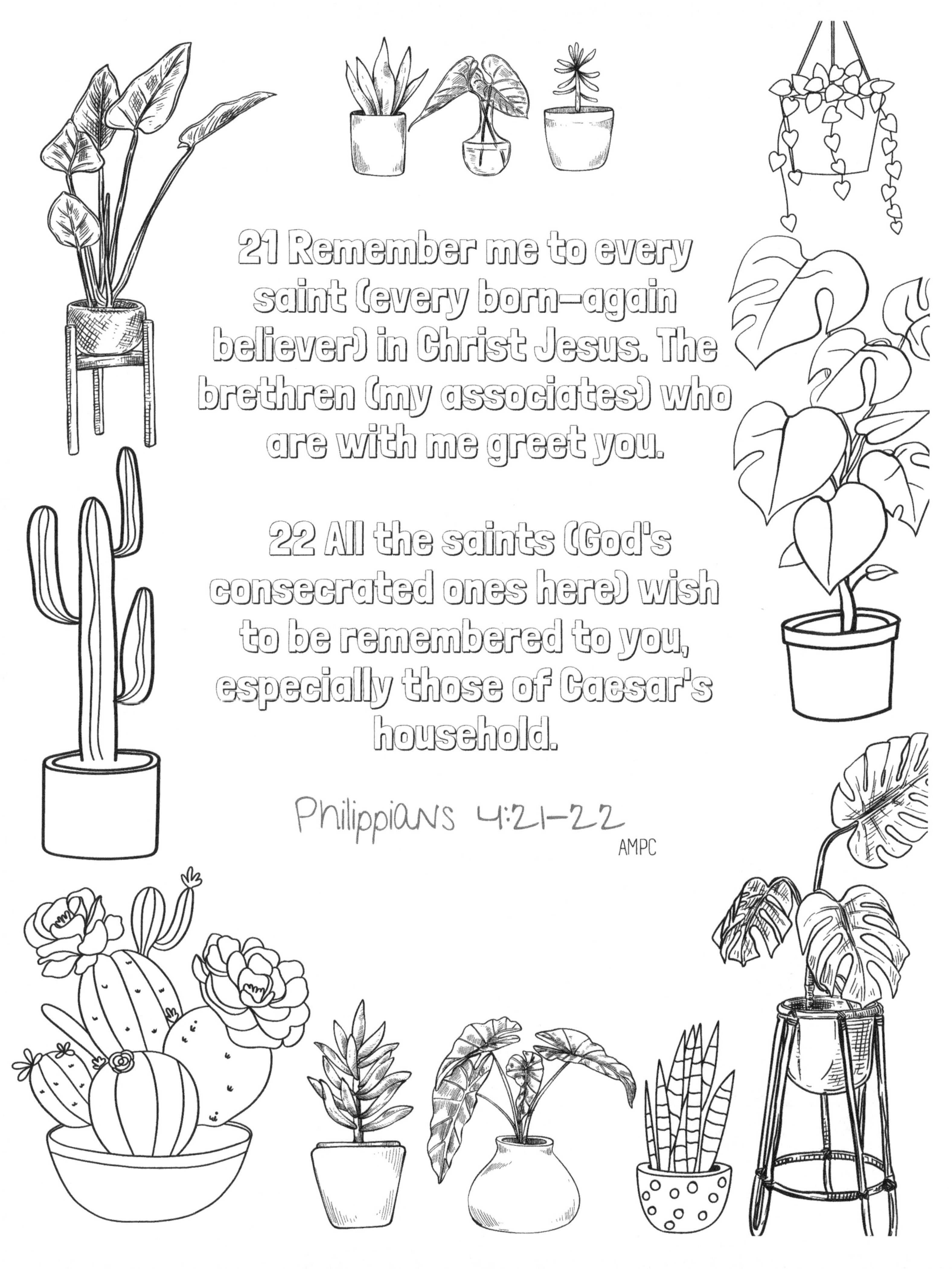
21 Remember me to every saint (every born-again believer) in Christ Jesus. The brethren (my associates) who are with me greet you.
22 All the saints (God's consecrated ones here) wish to be remembered to you, especially those of Caesar's household.
Philippians 4:21-22
AMPC

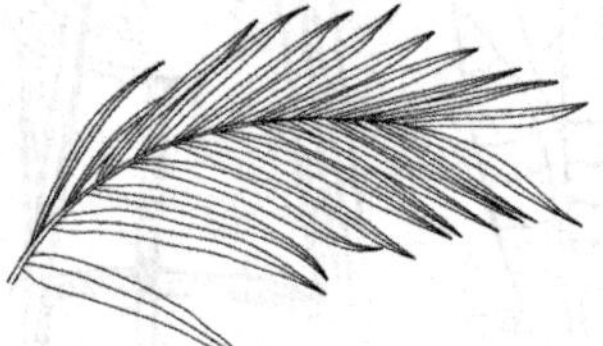

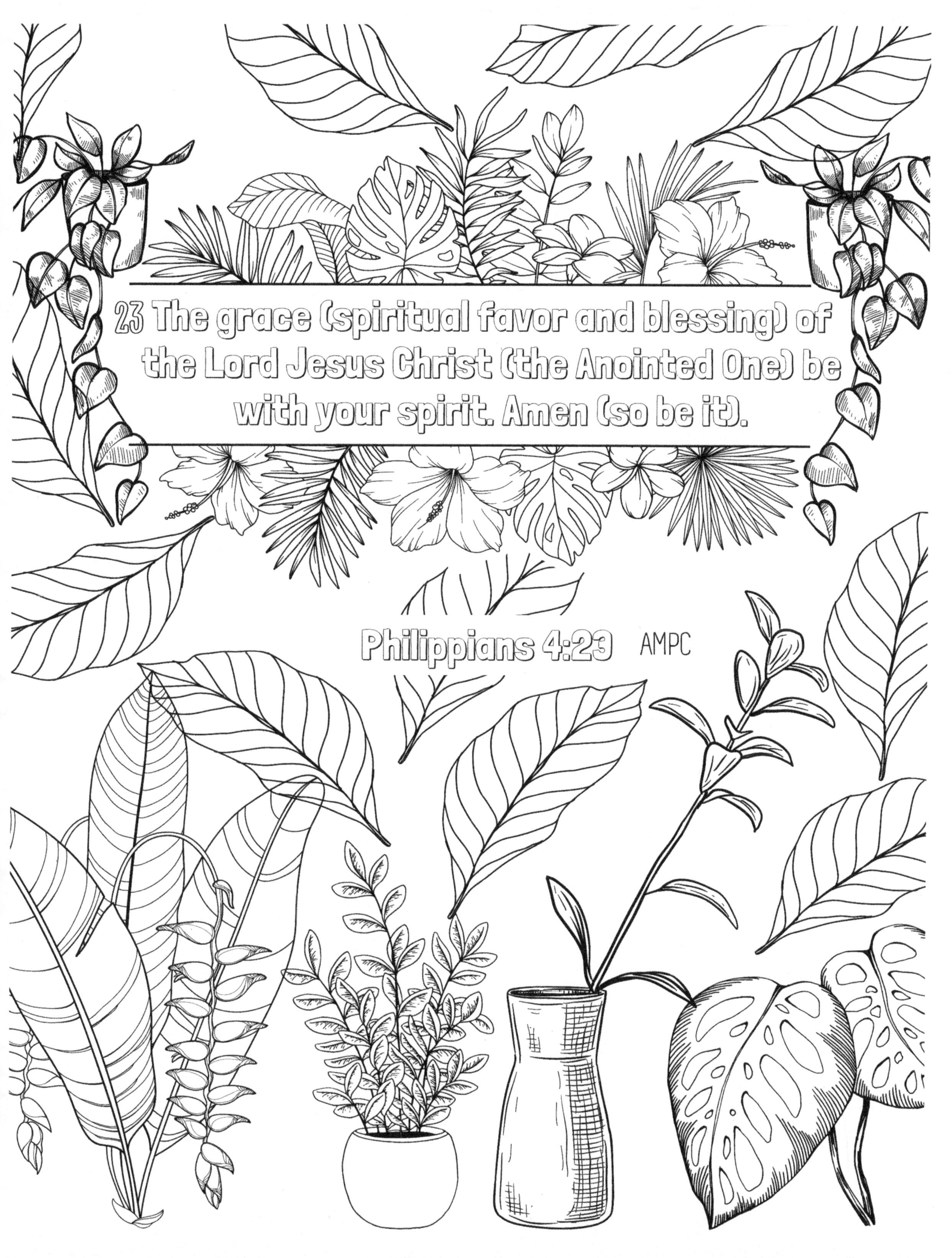
23 The grace (spiritual favor and blessing) of
the Lord Jesus Christ (the Anointed One) be
with your spirit. Amen (so be it).
Philippians 4:23 AMPC

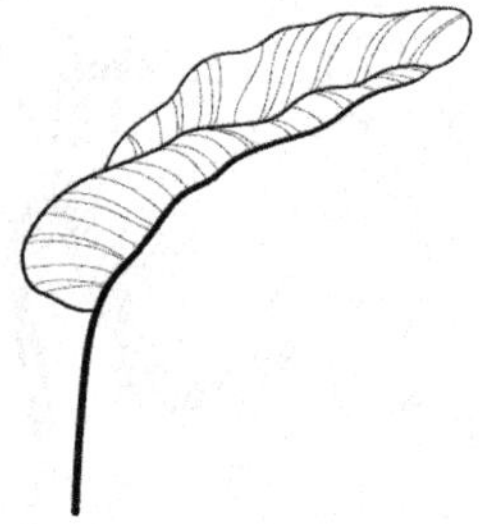

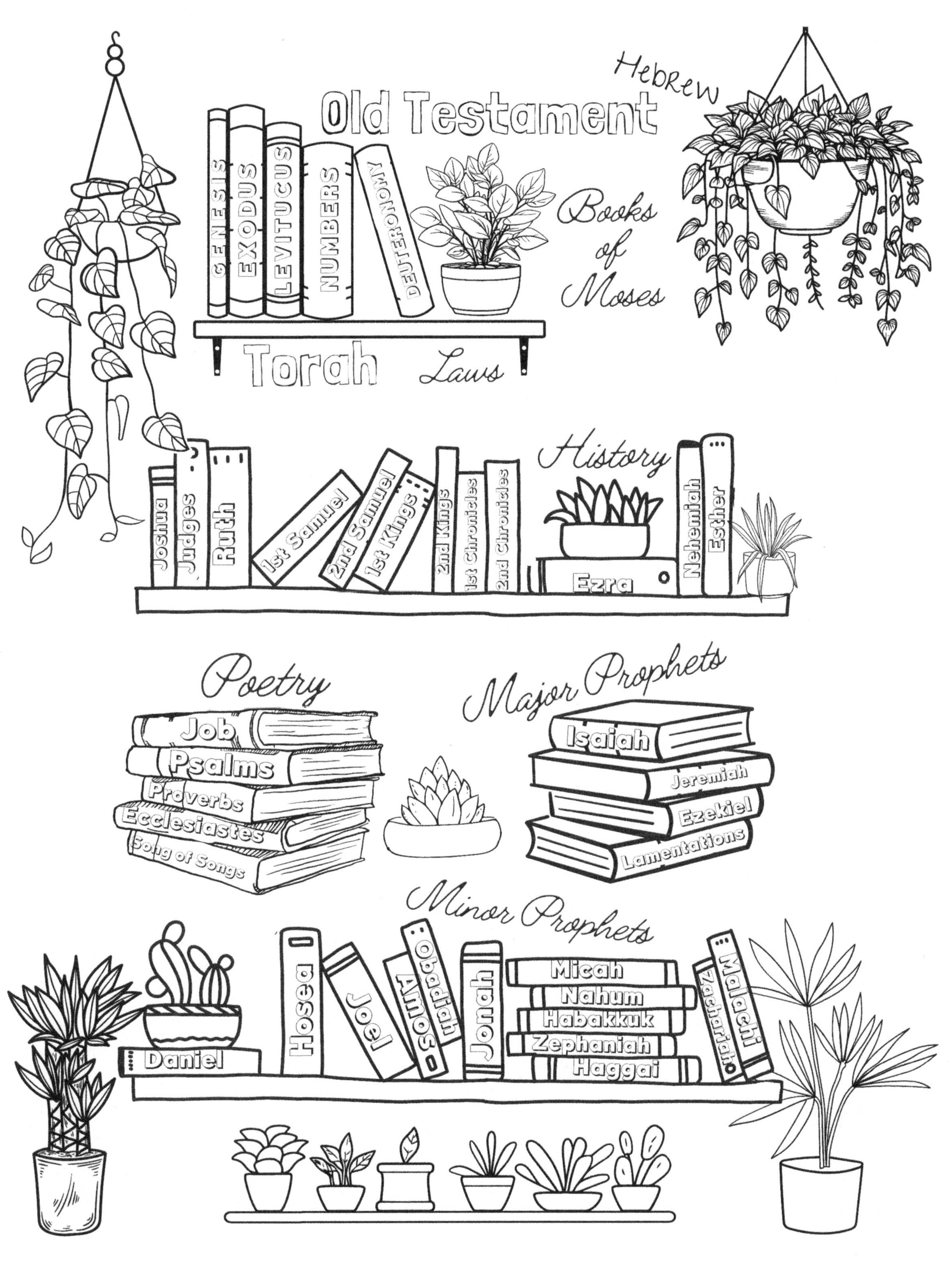
Hebrew
Old Testament
GENESIS
EXODUS
LEVITUCUS
NUMBERS
DEUTERONOMY
Books of Moses
Torah
Laws
History
Joshua
Judges
Ruth
1st Samuel
2nd Samuel
1st Kings
2nd Kings
1st Chronicles
2nd Chronicles
Ezra
Nehemiah
Esther
Poetry
Job
Psalms
Proverbs
Ecclesiastes
Song of Songs
Major Prophets
Isaiah
Jeremiah
Ezekiel
Lamentations
Minor Prophets
Daniel
Hosea
Joel
Amos
Obadiah
Jonah
Micah
Nahum
Habakkuk
Zephaniah
Haggai
Zechariah
Malachi

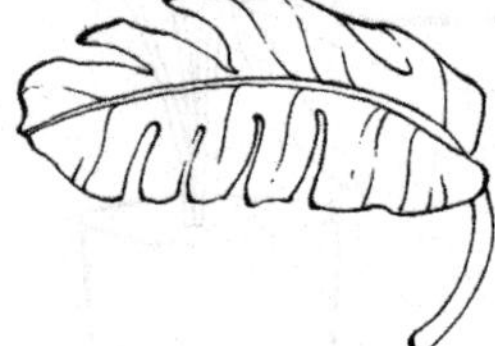

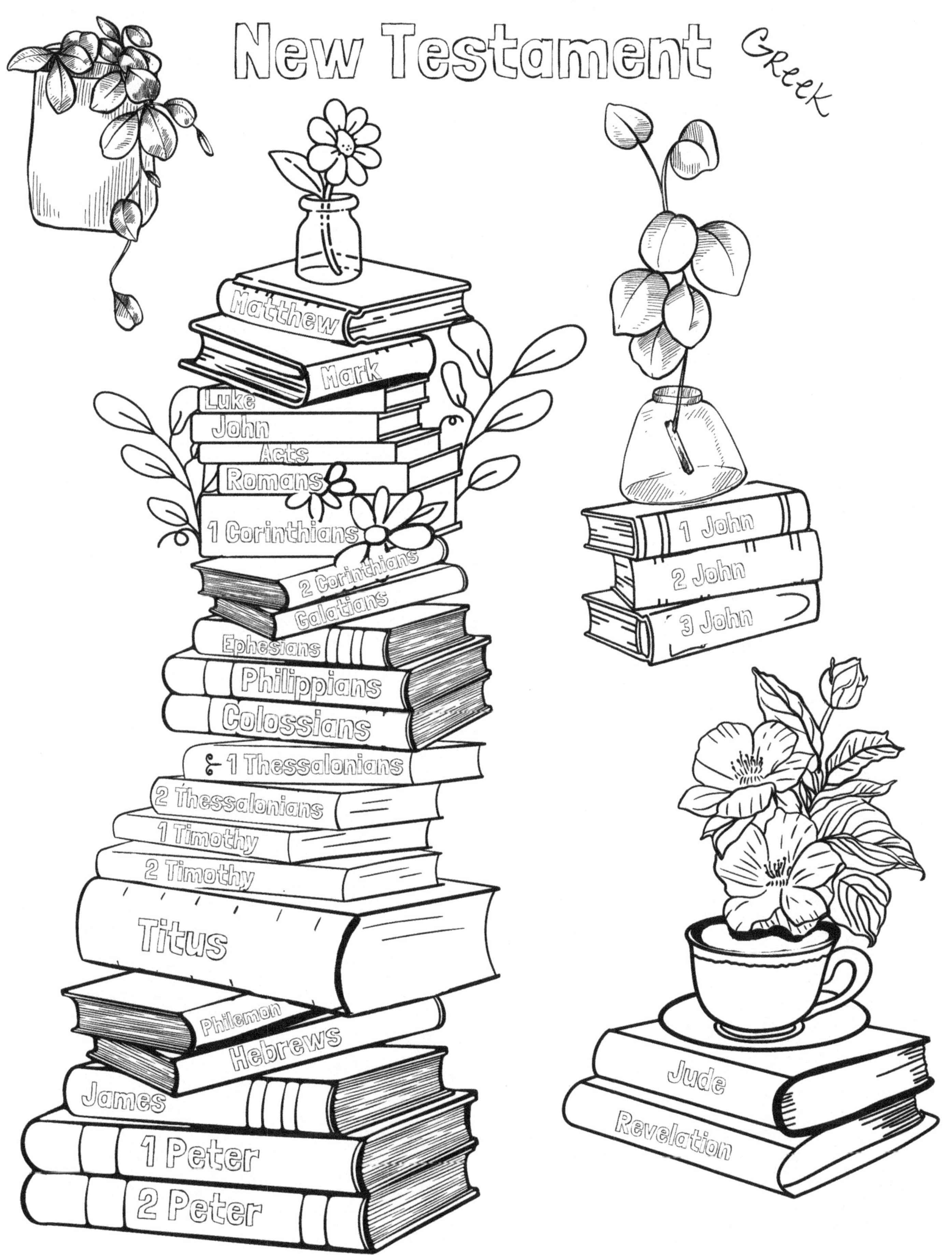
New Testament
Greek
Matthew
Mark
Luke
John
Acts
Romans
1 Corinthians
2 Corinthians
Galatians
Ephesians
Philippians
Colossians
1 Thessalonians
2 Thessalonians
1 Timothy
2 Timothy
Titus
Philemon
Hebrews
James
1 Peter
2 Peter
1 John
2 John
3 John
Jude
Revelation

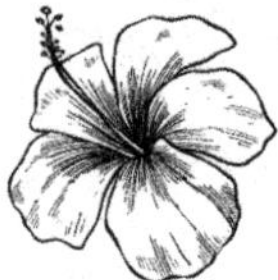

RESOURCES & TOPICS TO STUDY & DIG DEEPER INTO SCRIPTURE

HALLEY'S BIBLE HANDBOOK

BIBLEPROJECT.COM

ROMANS ROAD TO SALVATION

FRUITS OF THE SPIRIT

TEN COMMANDMENTS

STREETLIGHTS BIBLE AUDIO BIBLE TO BEATS.

SCRIPTURE LULLABIES. zzzz PEACEFUL SINGING SCRIPTURE TO SLEEP

STRONGS EXHAUSTIVE CONCORDANCE

BIBLE CONCORDANCE / LEXICONS

BLUE LETTER BIBLE

BIBLE HUB

NAME OF JESUS - MESSIAH - YHWH - YESHUA - ישוע - ISAIAH 9:6-7, 53

YESHAYAHU - 9:6-7, 53

THE GOSPEL OF JESUS CHRIST

HOLY SPIRIT

DEAD SEA SCROLLS

MASORETIC TEXT AND THE SEPTUAGINT

TANAKH / HABRIT HACHADASHA

ANCIENT HEBREW ALPHABET & THEIR NUMERIC VALUE

BIBLICAL HEBREW CALENDAR.

ANSWERSINGENESIS.ORG

2 Corinthians 5:17

John 14:6

Look up scripture in the Hebrew and Greek.
Old Testament-Hebrew
New Testament-Greek

John 3:16

Romans Road to Salvation

Romans 3:23,
Romans 6:23,
Romans 5:8,
Romans 10:9-10,
and Romans 10:13.

Ephesians 2:8

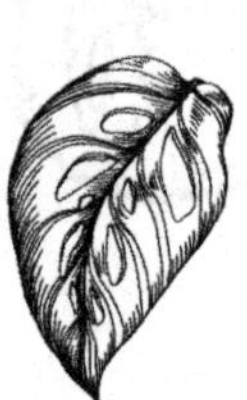

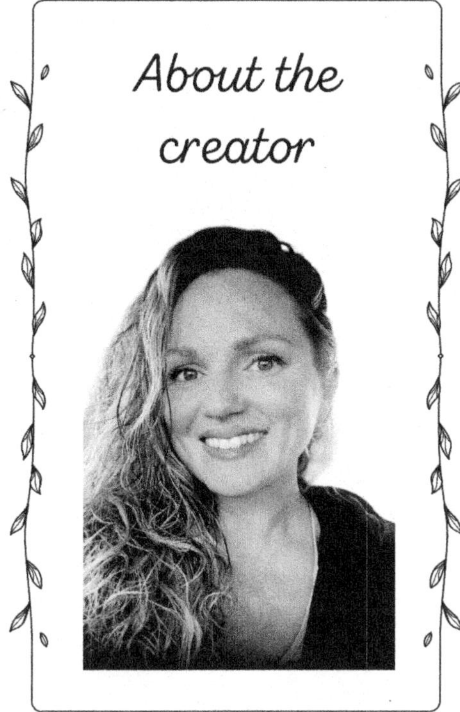

Amanda Kiser

Amanda Kiser is a Fine Art Painter, creativc, and entrepreneur. She loves to venture into visual arts, songwriting, writing books, graphic design and multiple art forms in her creative time with Papa God. Her paintings come from an intimate time hanging out with Yahweh King Jesus. She is passionate about being an artist but also a wife to her husband and a momma to her three boys. Her passion is to bring the heart of the Father God to people through the arts. To see people be healed set free and delivered by and through the love of God Adonai.

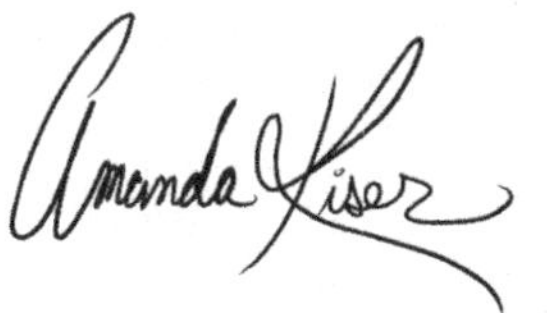

More of Amandas Creations

You can find many more of Amanda's creations to purchase via her Linktree site.

https://linktr.ee/amandakiserart

If you would like to be featured coloring this book, make sure to #

#BibleColorTherapy

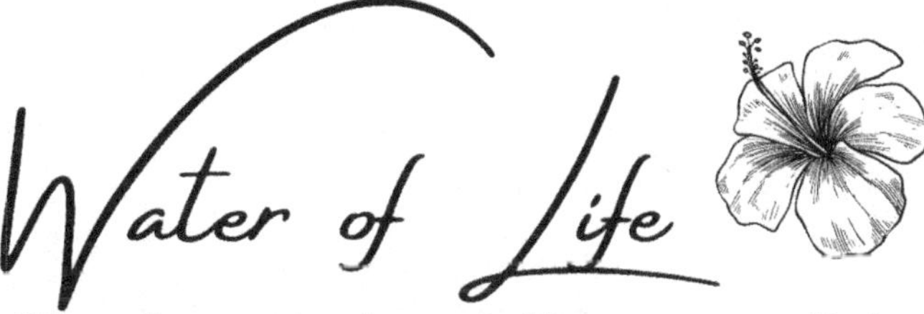

Oil on Canvas by Amanda Kiser

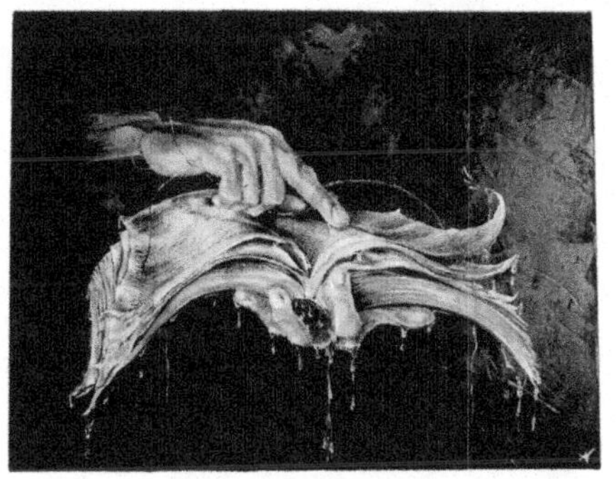

Prints of Water of Life

Jesus answered her, All who drink of this water will be thirsty again.
But whoever takes a drink of the water that I will give him shall never, no never, be thirsty any more. But the water that I will give him shall become a spring of water welling up (flowing, bubbling) [continually] within him unto (into, for) eternal life.
John 4:13-14

Now on the final and most important day of the Feast, Jesus stood, and He cried in a loud voice, If any man is thirsty, let him come to Me and drink!
He who believes in Me [who cleaves to and trusts in and relies on Me] as the Scripture has said, From his innermost being shall flow [continuously] springs and rivers of living water.
John 7:37-38

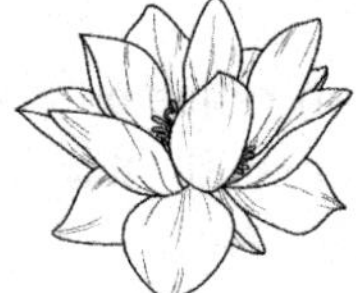

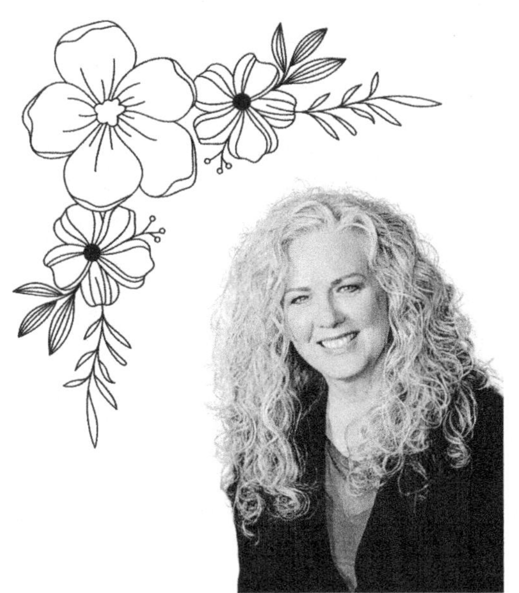

About the publisher

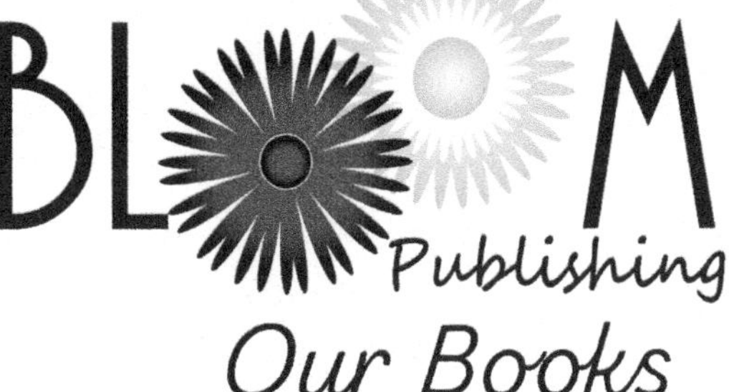
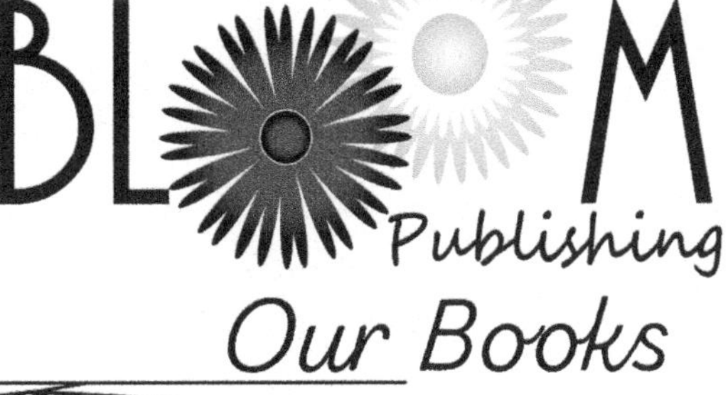

Our Books

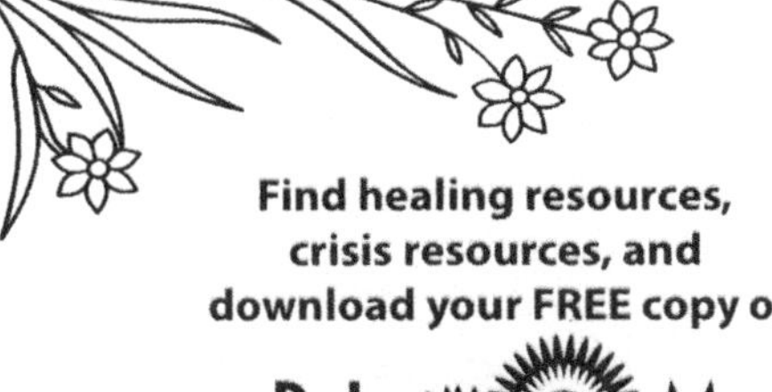

Find healing resources, crisis resources, and download your FREE copy of

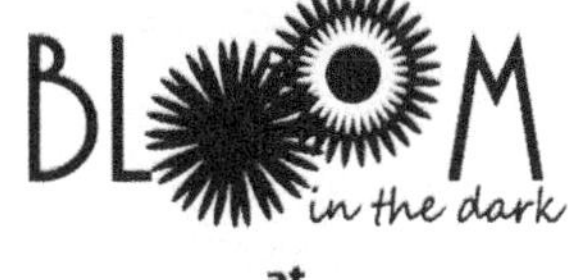

at

Bloominthedark.org/free-book

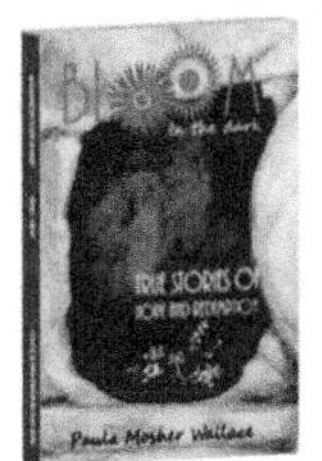

by
Paula Mosher Wallace
President of Bloom In The Dark, Inc.
paula@bloominthedark.com

A journal to renew your mind... one day at a time.

Use this 90 day devotional journal with assessments and daily questions will help you build new thought patterns, muscle memories, and neural pathways.

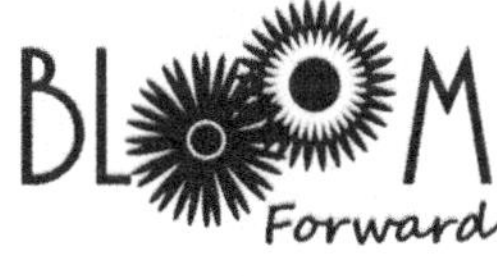

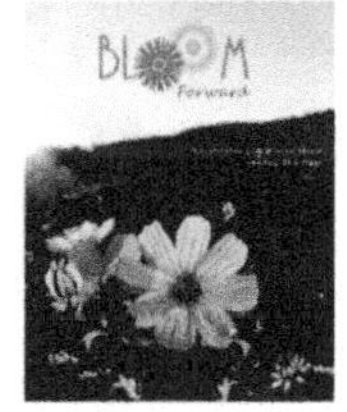

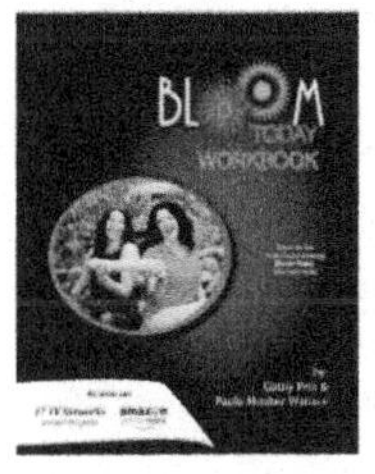

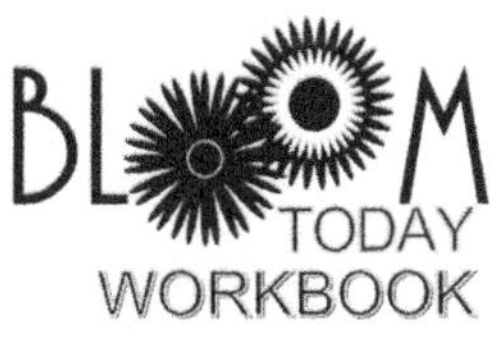

Videos & Coaching Tools
by
Ginny Priz & Paula Mosher Wallace
Based on the Bloom Today TV show

BloomTodayTV.com

A complex trauma recovery story...
Everyone can begin to heal by believing these core truths:

Core Truth 1	God designed me with a purpose in mind
Core Truth 2	I am not what has happened to me
Core Truth 3	Reinforced lies do not equal truth
Core Truth 4	Healing from trauma is possible
Core Truth 5	I am who God says I am
Core Truth 6	Helping others helps me

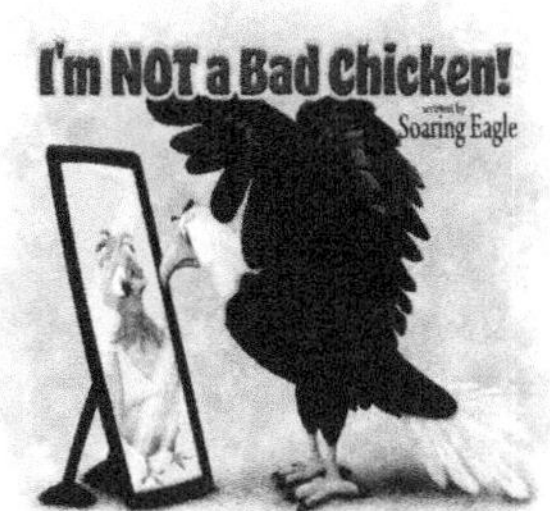

Paula Mosher Wallace

Best known for being the Founder of Bloom In The Dark, Inc., Paula Mosher Wallace is an Ex-Victim determined to use her story of complex trauma, CPTSD, and addiction recovery to help the hurting around the world. Born in a cult commune in Peru, Paula was horrifically abused by both genders beginning at age 2. The cycles of abuse lasted for 40 years. 17 years of intensive healing and recovery along with extensive training in trauma healing has established Paula as an international expert in the trauma healing and addiction recovery fields. As an ordained minister, trauma coach and media missionary, Paula shares healing and recovery stories and strategies with the world through mass media.

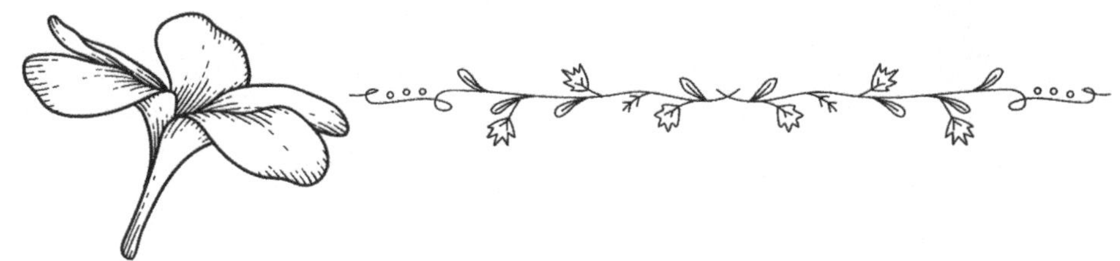

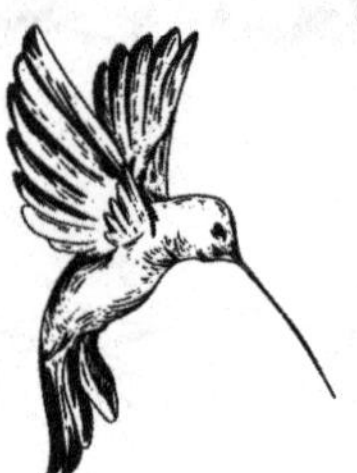

Certificate of Completion

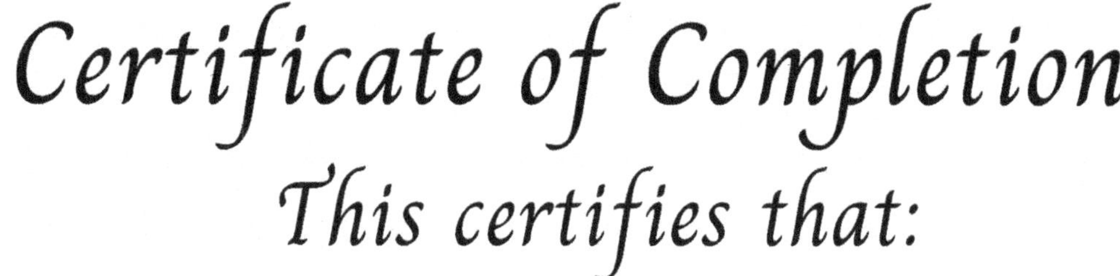

This certifies that:

____

Name

Successfully completed
Bible Color Therapy:
Philippians

Presented on the __________ Day of __________

In the year of __________

By

Paula Mosher Wallace

Amanda Kiser

Amanda Kiser

Made in the USA
Monee, IL
07 July 2026

56544782R00059